What does it mean to be 'Indian'?

S.N. BALAGANGADHARA
IN COLLABORATION WITH
SARIKA RAO

Notion Press Media Pvt Ltd

No. 50, Chettiyar Agaram Main Road,
Vanagaram, Chennai, Tamil Nadu – 600 095

First Published by Notion Press 2021
Copyright © S.N. Balagangadhara 2021
All Rights Reserved.

ISBN
Hardcase 978-1-68523-463-8
Paperback 978-1-68509-771-4

To

Quintus Aurelius Symmachus

The Last Pagan Prefect of Rome.

4th CE

CONTENTS

PREFACE

This book is for an intelligent but non-academic public. Unlike scholarly tracts, the book is not filled with footnotes or a bibliography and is not written in a technical or scholarly language. Despite this, it is not a work of fiction either. It may be less entertaining than a travelogue or a cookbook that you might pick up on the footpaths of our cities, in railway kiosks, and at airport booksellers. Such books will help you pass time in a pleasant fashion perhaps, but not this one. Here, you will need to spend time, quite some time in fact, if you want to think through the issues I raise. So, you are justified in asking why you should spend the time you do not have in reading this book, since you desperately need every little portion of that time to live a very busy life. In short: what makes this non-academic, non-fiction work worth reading?

In a sense, I can answer this question just as easily as you raise it: this book will satisfy the curiosity which its title generates. But this is not enough. Even if you are very curious (you must at least be reasonably curious; why otherwise would you pick up this book and come to read this preface?), how to persuade you that this is not an idle curiosity, which killed the cat? After reading this book, you will realize that your curiosity expresses a hunger to know, and that it is not idle. But how to persuade you of this before you have read this book? To do this, I must talk about the content and the goals of the book in this short preface and persuade you in the process that you are hungry to know, and that you will find a decent meal in this book to satisfy that hunger.

I will do that by focussing on your concerns. If what you seek is knowledge, how might I make sure that you acquire it? In general terms: what does it mean to transmit knowledge to those who want and also deserve it?

Consider the issue of transmitting knowledge to non-specialists, lay persons and to all others interested in it. Today, in the West, people refer to this in terms of 'popularizing science'. Programmes and projects attempting this are well funded. Some Indians enthusiastically go this way: they too want a 'science for the people'. However, this book does not 'popularize'. How, then, can it fulfil its goal of satisfying the hunger to know without becoming a specialized tract?

To answer this question, we must figure out what popularization of science could possibly mean. If we accept the idea that science is the best example of knowledge we have, its popularization means its 'vulgarization'. Or, to use the American phrase, we must 'dumb it down'. However, knowledge, when dumbed down or vulgarized, ceases to be knowledge. It loses its status as science or knowledge. For instance, evolutionary theory is often presented in a popularized way with the claim that the descent of human beings can be traced back to apes. In such a case, neither the teaching nor a propagation of evolutionary theory occurs. The simian descent of humankind is a factoid that cannot be considered a scientific theory if presented in that form. Such a dumbed down idea, a factoid in fact, is easily met with a facile retort such as "you might be proud to say that your grandfather is a monkey, but mine was not", or "God created the original parents", or something to that effect. This is not a Science versus Religion controversy, but a dispute that comes into being when knowledge is dumbed down, popularized, or vulgarized. We cannot transmit knowledge in this fashion. All we can do is deform it and sell it as a collection of factoids. This partially explains why people are so scientifically illiterate in the US today, despite massive efforts to popularize science. This is the reason why 'alternative facts' become rivals to scientific claims; and why some people want to prevent babies from being vaccinated against diseases like polio and measles.

Around two thousand or more years ago, Indians too confronted this question: How to bring knowledge to the people? Even though I will speak neither in the book nor in this preface about how Indian culture solved this problem, I will say the following: Indian culture transmitted knowledge without popularizations, vulgarizations and without dumbing down ideas. The issue is not about how to popularize knowledge but how to make it maximally accessible to people.

This book stands firmly rooted in that Indian tradition which transmits knowledge without either popularizing it or dumbing it down, but by trying to reach those who seek to know. The strategy is to latch onto the hunger for knowledge present in people and to feed that hunger. This requires repetition of ideas in many ways and multiple forms; it means looking at thoughts from multiple perspectives and weaving as rich a pattern as possible. Therefore, this book does not differentiate axioms from premises; it does not build hypotheses and construct proofs or assemble evidence to support my theses. Thus, the book is non-academic. But it will make you think by tickling your brain and triggering the processes required for knowledge to emerge in you. I promise you that you will acquire it, if you are prepared to think; it is here that I intend this book to play a role.

By speaking of two cultures, Indian and Western, I have also indicated what this book does. It tackles the question formulated in the title of the book by talking about Western and Indian culture, and the influences generated by the first on the second. It shares with you the unvarnished results of more than four decades of scientific research without trivializing, vulgarizing, or dumbing down ideas. It is aimed at an intelligent if hungry public.

You, who are reading this preface, should therefore know that I see you as hungry for knowledge. All I can offer you is food for your brain. The same way the digestive organs must perform their functions in order to absorb food, your brain too must become cognitively busy to digest this book. Accept the gift if you are both hungry and deserving of this gift. It is true you will have to 'bend your back' to make your brain work, but I promise you a truly sumptuous meal.

Acknowledgement of help that we have received in this process is due now: we would like to thank the Aarohi Research Foundation, Bengaluru, for creating the necessary data and documentation for this work to enable the publication of this research through their project from Mythic society. Acknowledgements are also due to the Mythic Society, Bengaluru, for facilitating this work through Aarohi. Without their help and encouragement, we could not have written this book.

I would like to acknowledge my indebtedness to Venkateswara Reddy. Without his selfless labour lasting more than a decade, this book would be a 'never-was'.

And then there are two very, very special people I want to thank: there is Sarika Rao, who is as much responsible for this book as I am. However, she refuses to be named the co-author despite truly and really being one. Even though she is my niece in terms of our bloodlines, she is the daughter I never had.

And there is HQ, the one with many names, who is a 10 year old budding artist known as Hasse in Belgium and Hamsa in India. My wife very quickly convinced me into becoming her doting grandfather. When you look at the cover art, which she designed on her own after briefly listening to a short summary of the content, I hope you can guess why she is and remains my princess.

To these two, my enormous gratitude. They make an old man's life worth living. Thus 'gods' have gifted me with three diamonds: my wife, my stolen daughter and my princess. What good fortune, I ask myself often, has made me a deserving person for these three exceptional jewels?

Balu

July 2021

Ghent, Belgium

INTRODUCTION

Imagine, if you will, Indian culture as a single entity (in the neuter gender) consisting of Indians as its members. Imagine too that one day this culture realized that it was not sure about the nature of the inhabited world. Where and what is its place in the world? What should it do? How should it adapt and what would adaptation mean in this context? The time-tested way to find answers is through experimentation: to try out this or that strategy, develop new things as and when needed. Only its members can help; only they can do the experiments and be the experimental subjects. Let us agree not to ask questions about how this culture came to this realization and let there be no dispute about the dating of this event – India's independence from the British. Thus, this entity, Indian culture, takes to *massive experimentation* by telescoping events that took many decades to happen elsewhere in the world into happenings of a single decade, at times even less. Let us chronicle some of these experiments.

First, it takes to 'socialisms' of many kinds: Nehruvian socialism, the socialism of Lohia and the different socialisms of the Communist parties of India. Even as these experiments are initiated, this culture begins exploring *their limits*. The Naxalites from Andhra and the ML movement in Bengal impact India's youth in different parts of India and both socialisms (of Lohia and of Nehru) begin to crack under the pressure of events that, in the late 60's, led people elsewhere in the world to discover 'student power'. Many activist youth groups emerge in different parts of India, born outside the existing left, but already radicalized. Just as these groups seem to run out of steam, Indian culture pauses, as though considering, and plunges into another massive experimentation: the 'Dalit' movements and the 'secessionist' movements that do not pit the bourgeoisie against the proletariat, but social and cultural groups against each other. Even as they impact Indian culture through reservation policies and the contraction of the living space for some of India's children, a new experiment is initiated – it is time for the *Ratha Yatra* and the subsequent demolition of Babri Masjid. This experiment is still ongoing and even as it does, this entity launches yet another event with no parallels in human history. Indian culture sends two million or more of its people to the USA. This peacetime event is no exodus and much less an exile, even if some people insist on speaking of the 'Indian Diaspora'. (The Jewish Diaspora from where this word is borrowed refers to the periodic exiles of the Jewish people and their attempts at exodus and migration to other lands including India, to escape persecutions and pogroms that their past is so deeply scarred with.)

Some of India's children continue with these experiments; some have ceased doing so. What has Indian culture learned through these experiments? Either that some of the answers proved to be no answers at all or, at best, only partial ones. Is India socialist? Is it the proletariat? Or, perhaps, the landless peasant? Or by gendering it now: Is she the Dalit, or merely the woman? Has she always been a Sikh, a Tamil or a Marathi, and never a single entity? Is she a 'Hindu', a Muslim, a member of the Christian flock or merely, but always truly 'secular'?

India, it appears, has been interrogating herself through all these experiments: *Who is she?* This is no third-rate 'identity politics' taught in Chicago or Columbia by the post-colonials, but the strivings of a culture. We, her children, express this striving as well. Whatever our individual motives, however varied our individual biographies, today, we too are asking the question: *What is it to be 'Indian'*? However, when we ask this question, we do not seek our 'identities', whatever that word may mean in the multiple ways it is used today. By the time you have finished with this book, you will know what we are seeking.

India did not merely retrace past events from elsewhere. She also portends the future: 'the woke and the social justice warriors', who plague the intellectual and social world today in the West were birthed in India more than half a century ago. The very same people (from the left and the right) who cheered and egged on such warriors in India at one time, realize dimly now that this phenomenon is poison in the entrails of a society and a culture. But, in its blindness, the West does not yet see that its future is clearly delineated and foregrounded in this slice of the Indian past. India's social and cultural situation of today etches with unmistakable clarity the future that nations face when they sell 'identity politics' on a massive scale. The chickens they forced India to breed have now come home to the West to roost.

However, much like her, we cannot reject the past: without it, we would not be who we are any more. Nor can we turn our backs to the present: this is where we must live. Our future will partly depend upon how we make use of our past and present. And what we will remember of our past and present is partly defined by the future we want. Thus, this attempt requires that our cultural past talks in the language of the present; but that, I have discovered, is *the* task for the future. At this moment, however, we must become aware that *we* are asking this question and that the answer *matters* to each one of us.

Why ask this question today? Do we not know the answers? After all, a lot is written about India, her culture, her past, her society, the psychology and sociology of individuals and their groups. Why is this not enough to answer the query about what it means to be 'Indian'? Why the need for all that experimentation?

It is because what we have learnt about ourselves so far, let me call it 'the received view', is either false or very fragmentary. Whether we claim that India is a class society or a caste society or a combination of both, we are not saying very much. Such a claim merely tells us that India too has a society ('India is a caste society', as they say), and that it either fully ('we only have classes in our society') or partially ('in Indian society, classes and castes are mixed') mirrors other societies and people one way or another. Our question is not whether we are also human beings, or whether we also have a social and cultural life, but what kind of people we are, where we have come from and where we should be heading as a society, as a culture and as individuals. Thus, we ask: what does it mean to be 'Indian'? We are taught to scare quote 'Indian', having been educated into believing that we are not yet a nation and having been taught that India was never a monolithic culture. It is not sophisticated, chic, cool, or 'scientific' to foreground 'Indian' without registering reservations regarding the use of this word. Thus, we feel compelled to scare quote 'Indian', lest, as educated city-folk, we come across as uncultivated and illiterate village-folk. Besides, if we desire the scientific spirit, we are repeatedly told we must be wary of 'Hindu nationalism'. After all, reasonable people have eschewed 'Hinduism' and, in this day and age, one should definitely not become a 'Hindu fundamentalist'. This is the received view.

Thus forewarned, let us pursue the question of being 'Indian' and find out what it will take to answer this question. Here the response is easy: *a collective effort.* What does such an effort entail? In answering this question, I want to share my reflections on this task, which I have been pursuing for nearly four decades now.

The first step, quite obviously, calls for spreading awareness about how India has been represented and understood so far. This entails finding *people* willing to challenge the received view, and actively *supplant* it. This requires producing literature of two sorts: (a) the debunking kind; and (b) that which provides new and novel conceptualizations of different aspects of Indian culture. This means that serious and systematic research must be undertaken by many different people on many different themes. My knowledge of the intellectual scene tells me that there are very few such people. So, one must look to *recruit* younger, gifted people willing to do such research.

For this to happen, we need three things: (a) an intellectual visibility and social respectability required to attract excellent young minds for this research; (b) a system of rewards and incentives that makes it worthwhile for them to pursue such research for decades; (c) a *training* not only in doing such research, but also in publishing its results in highly visible scientific journals and as books with serious content. We need to do all these three things for these young minds to succeed in becoming 'public' intellectuals.

Parallel to these, there is the mammoth task of planting these seeds in the Indian soil itself.

Can this be done? I believe so. We have all the resources we need: people who can strategize; those who can build organizations; those who can raise finances; those who can go straight to the heart of a problem and represent it in simple terms; those who anticipate and formulate central questions for enquiry; and, above all, an interested and concerned audience.

India, today, is at a crossroads: she has been at many such crossroads in the past, and she will be facing many more in the future. Neither of these issues is relevant to us because we can make a *difference* only to this one. We have the people. We have the brains. We have the talent. We have the energy. We have the money. We have the instruments, the knowledge, and the abilities. We have the capacity to create the know-how as we work on the project. What more do we need?

I think our culture is going to see a renaissance. Such a renaissance is of importance not just to us, Indians, but also to all of humankind. Because this is going to lay the real foundation for the sciences of the social, it will provide a surprising answer to the question, 'what does it mean to be 'Indian'?' This process is going to take place – sooner, if we accelerate the pace; later, if we do nothing about it. In the latter case, this may not happen in your lifetime or mine; but happen it shall. Of this, I am utterly convinced. It is this conviction that has kept me going all these years; it is the same conviction that has made me want to reach out to you.

CHAPTER 1

ACCESSING OUR PAST

We, Indians, are the products of two colonialisms: the Islamic and the British. This claim may generate puzzlement or objection, or both: true, the Moghuls and the British conquered us, but did a religion (Islam) colonize us? How can a religion colonize a people, unless in terms of a total conversion? Even then, how accurate is it to label the religious process of conversion as colonization, especially considering that Indians did not become Muslims *en masse*? Though important, I will not answer these questions at this stage. I will come back to them later. For now, let us reserve this as an oddity in our minds. A religion (Islam) and a people (the British) colonized us, Indians. True, we were overrun by many conquerors, but we were not colonized by them all. Colonization, as many have shown, is not merely a process of conquering territories, occupying peoples, and extracting revenues. It goes deeper. It is not just about colonizing the mind of a people by making them 'dream' that they too could become 'modern', developed and sophisticated someday. Nor is it a question of merely imitating the colonizers, trying to become like them. It is deeper than all of these. It is an inhumane process that involves violence of all sorts – from the purely physical to the entirely psychic. Colonialism alters the way we look at the world and it displaces native ways of experiencing the world through sheer violence. *It is a process of denying to peoples and cultures their own experiences; of making them aliens to themselves; of actively preventing descriptions of*

their experiences except in terms defined by the colonizers. The terms of these descriptions prevent the 'native' from discovering himself. To the colonized, there is no simple or naive return to the lost world. Colonization changes his world forever. Though reprehensible and tragic, this is what colonialism does, and we need to understand this truth about ourselves in the first place. (There is another substantial issue that I cannot address in this chapter and that relates to why we, Indians, continue to be colonized when the actual event ended more than seventy years ago.)

However, understanding this truth requires multiple threads, different combinations, and many complex clusters. Like the epic Mahabharata, it can be told in fragments, beginning at multiple points, and by focussing on different storylines. So, let us begin somewhere and see where the story takes us. Because we are talking about stories, why not begin with questions about what stories are?

Under colonial rule, the British aggressively pushed their beliefs onto us. They quizzed us about our past in ways we were not used to. Taking our multiple stories, epics, and puranas, as though they were historiographies, they derided us for believing in their 'truth'. The story about our intellectuals under colonial rule is a sad tale of succumbing to what they did not understand. But concealing ignorance under a swagger, they broadly took one of the two paths available to them. Either they denied the truth of our stories about the past or attempted to show that these stories are 'true' chronicles of our past. It did not occur to our intellectuals to study the colonizer's culture to figure out the nature of the questions they encountered. They believed, without knowing why, that the thoughts, behaviour and attitudes of the British colonial masters exemplified reason, rationality and scientificity. This belief induced the swagger. Thus, in the *first phase*, our intellectuals accepted the absence of historiography in our culture and set out to solve multiple lacunae by writing empirical histories of India. These were based on the 'philosophy of history' that the Europeans were peddling on the Asian sub-continent at steeply discounted prices. In the *second phase*, they joined the Europeans in deriding Indian culture and our rich stock of stories about the past. In the *third phase*, they took over the European historiography of India and went on to garnish it with Indian spices, which merely meant adding new 'factual details', as and when one 'discovered' them. In this sense, the attitude of writing a history of Indian culture and civilization, based on a meticulous 'study' of the past is nothing new. It is an old knee-jerk reaction to the Protestant critique of Indian culture and her traditions.

What do these historiographies accomplish? They teach us, for instance, that the Mahabharata war could have factually taken place, except that, of course, it was probably a war between coalitions of tribes. Poetic exaggeration merely gave us descriptions of epic proportions. So, in all probability, these historians assure us, there was a war, somewhere in the north of India about a few thousand years ago. As far as Krishna lifting the mountain with his little finger, or Ghatotkacha fighting in the Mahabharata war with the 'magic' of the Rakshasas, they do not even bother to hide their contempt: of course, it is either all nonsense or mere exaggeration. Surely we know that no human individual can lift a mountain with his little finger and, in all probability, the Rakshasas were just the name of some existing tribe that, perhaps, was neutral in this tribal war. In other words, the Mahabharata, the Ramayana, and all our stories about the past are merely disguised historiographies, or exaggerations and lies penned by our incompetent ancestors. Incompetent because they could not even accomplish what Thucydides the Greek did, or what the Chinese did so many thousands of years ago, which only the current generation of historians can decipher. At least, this is what we are told.

This group of historians shared the deep, Nehruvian contempt for India, her culture and her traditions. They strutted around in the enclaves of elite universities, flew to international conferences to present their papers, and felt they were much above the rest of the Indian masses steeped in ignorance and superstition. Unaware of their own profound ignorance of the origin, nature, and meaning of these 'scientific' questions, our historians were content to reproduce whatever their Metropolitan masters desired. They had built a wall of separation between their 'secularism' and the 'religiosity' of the Indian masses. This was received very well: didn't one of the founding fathers of the American constitution urge creating a 'wall of separation' between the religiosity of the masses and the State? Drawing such parallels won the enthusiastic applause of and plaudits from the patriotic Americans present in these international conferences, which is what these intellectuals sought. Never mind that it did not help Indians understand their past any better than before. That issue never worried our intellectuals in any case.

Both British liberalism and Nehruvian secularism brought forth another form of reaction in India. We have just been introduced to the first kind – the one that derides Indian culture, her traditions and holds the West as the picture of perfection. Such people dominate the media and the universities, as they have done for centuries. But it has generated an antipode, another tendency, which too is a child of British Protestantism and thus Christian to the core, but one which borrows from other strands available in Western Christianity.

This tendency attempts to go the other way: it claims that our stories about the past are *literally* our histories. We too had historiographers in the past; we too know 'the truth' about our past; our stories give us the literal 'truth' about our past; they are not poetic lies or exaggerations. Enter the *Sangh Parivar*.

As I see it, the Sangh Parivar is an organizational umbrella that houses and animates many different organizations, both big and small. At its core, it is cadre-based much the same way the communist parties once were. However, unlike them, the Sangh Parivar is not a political organization and it has also been able to grow both as an organization and evolve into an expanding movement. As an entity that is both an organization and a movement, it houses a complex collection of people with rich interactional patterns among themselves. In many senses, it mirrors the culture it is born in wonderfully well. In terms of an analogy, if you ask a hundred Indians why they do Ganesha Puja, you are likely to get ninety if not a hundred answers. The people in Sangh Parivar can be likened to this analogy. Even though they belong to the Sangh Parivar and listen to their leaders and follow their organizational heads faithfully, the answer to the question why they do so is extremely pluriform. It also contains and expresses many tendencies about its course, lines of development, and its future. In the case of the Sangh Parivar, sustaining this diversity and multiplicity is a *sine qua non* for its continued existence as the largest *civil* organization in the second most populous country in the world. As someone looking from the outside with no experience in this organization, I would like to *locate* this extraordinary variety that the Sangh Parivar is within the culture in which it is born. This pluriform Parivar can be *generically* characterized in this way. It intuitively reacts to the prevailing descriptions of Indian culture. It senses profundity and depth in Indian culture, her traditions, her multiple stories about the past, and so on. It senses too that there are various ways of being on earth and that the Christian and the Muslim ways of 'being-in-the-world' are but two out of many such ways. It reacts with incomprehension while listening to criticism of virtually everything Indian by the religiously founded 'secular' thinking. Why secular thinking is religiously founded, would require a digression so I will set that aside for now. The Sangh Parivar resonates very,

very deeply with the images and metaphors expressed in a cultural vocabulary that is Indian to the core and to the practices and the traditions that express these, such as festivals and celebrations. Despite this, when characterized in terms of its *intellectual repertoire,* it is handicapped by a profound and deep ignorance of Western culture. But this shortcoming is something it shares with Nehruvian and other secularisms, liberals, Marxists, post-colonials and so on. All of them share the same heraldry, which is that they are children of colonialisms. As such, they suffer from the same handicap: for centuries, India has been unable to produce truly towering intellectuals of international stature.

This is surprising but, in some sense, also predictable. In this culture, knowledge has a status rivalled by none. Knowledge trumps truth in our culture. The acquisition of knowledge overshadows 'the search for truth', which is of supreme value in Western culture. It is alleged that Indians have 33 crores of gods, but there is no 'god' or 'goddess' of truth. The goddess Saraswathi embodies knowledge, not truth. Contrast this with the Semitic religions: God is the Truth (not knowledge, *nota bene*). Hence, it is *surprising* that we have not *systematically* produced and sustained world class intellectuals.

Our 'secular' intellectuals reproduce staid jargons they learnt from the West in tiring ways: if the hundredth version of the Lockean 'original' contract gets written by the liberals, the progressives read them in an 'original position' but under the Rawlsian 'veil of ignorance'; Gramscian 'organic' but Marxist intellectuals with Parisian Althusserian undertones are enthused by the 'tendency of the rate of profit to fall'; while Said's 'worked over' critique of Orientalism thrills post-colonial souls, the postmodernists are ecstatic about rediscovering the relation between the 'originary' violence and Law. And I have not mentioned the Foucauldian in the Delhi Dhaba.

Within the ambit of the above, the criticisms of the Sangh Parivar take *predictable* forms. Martin Marty's massively funded Chicago Fundamentalism Project's results are heard in the Indian university halls and in *Indian Express* columns expressing moral indignations about 'Hindu fundamentalism'. Both the criticism of 'Hinduism' and its 'defence' have been rehearsed during the British Raj a million times over. But each teller of the tale thinks s/he is being 'original'. In any case, it is within this framework that a second tendency arises in Indian culture.

The diametrically opposed stance to British liberalism and Nehruvian secularism is a *mere antipode* and is easily *domesticated*. Its antipodal existence is due to the absence of native intellectuals over the centuries. If such intellectuals existed, neither the Indian repetitions of liberal criticism nor an antipodal defence would have been necessary. Now, both are on the menu. However, by legitimizing the questions of history raised by these liberal and secular intellectuals, the antipodal stance gets absorbed as another child of British Protestantism, Christian to the core, but one which borrows from other strands available in Western Christianity.

Such a tendency that opposes the dominant centuries-old story merely claims that epics about the past are *literally* our histories. Then, it would look as though we too have had historiographers in the past; we too would then know 'the truth' about our past; our stories would also chronicle our past without being exaggerations or poetic lies. Why would discovering such 'competent' historical writings in our epics not solve our problems? Because, even if such a claim solves one kind of a problem, it does so by generating a whole host of other problems. Let me explain.

Note that our multiple stories about the past, among other things, provide us with a deep connection to our collective past. We read or hear the Mahabharata and the Ramayana and feel that Rama,

Duryodhana, Dharmaraja, etc. were our kings. When we participate in the festival of Deepavali, we open our doors to Bali, a *rakshasa*, as the greatest king we ever had. We feel connected to Sita, Draupadi and Abhimanyu. We weep on hearing the story of Ekalavya; we are touched by Karna's fate; we get angry at Shakuni and Dushasana. We very much want brothers to be like Rama and Lakshmana. We feel *connected to all these people* in a myriad of ways and these connections are deeper than our connections to our great grandfathers, whom we have never met in all probability. In short, we feel we are a part of that genealogy which these multiple *stories present as our collective past.*

This collective past has a rich and varied tapestry: it carries sounds of *Ik onkaar* from a gurudwara that touch an inner chord; it includes the *Dargah* at the Baba Budangiri that evokes a familiar sense of reverence; it sings the songs of Shishunala Sharif that carry an identifiably Indian content. It is this past that makes us light candles at the Infant Jesus Church, drape Mother Mary of Velankanni with a silk saree and listen to the Church sermons with the wonder with which we take in multiple *sthalapuranas*. Events like colonization that gave birth to such attitudes constitute our past, live on in the present, and indicate the direction of a possible future.

As children, we have often wondered where some people from our stories lived and what languages they spoke. Did Krishna speak a language other than Sanskrit, was it a local 'dialect' or something else? When Yaksha challenged Dharmaraja, was it in Sanskrit, 'the language of the gods', or another one? In which language did Hanumantha speak to Sita, when he decided not to speak in Sanskrit, because of the fear that she would think that he is Ravana in disguise if he spoke in Sanskrit? In which language did the rishis and the kings from Khamboja communicate with those from Jambudweepa? Are the Nagas of today's India also the descendants of Arjuna? Is the Mathura near Delhi also the place where Krishna lived? Are the

Vaanaras that helped Rama also the ancestors of those monkeys that we see today? And the *Yugas*, what are they exactly? Are the *treta* and the *dwapara yugas* merely how the earth was so many hundreds of thousands of years ago? And so on and so forth.

As we grew up and learnt our geographies and sciences, we did try to combine both: how could there be *treta yuga* when our species is hardly 300,000 years old? How could Bhima really have the strength of 10,000 elephants and Duryodhana merely 9999? How could Dharmaraja walk to *Swarga* and, if he did, why could Trishanku not do the same? *Etcetera.* We went to our elders with these questions, and their answers, though no answers at all, satisfied us. Over time, we stopped asking these questions. Not because we knew the answers or because these questions are unanswerable. We stopped asking such questions because we learnt that *these were not the right questions to ask.* Finally, we assumed an indifferent attitude to the facticity of these stories.

To grow up as an Indian is to learn that these stories should be treated differently than the claims from our geography lessons. We do not look at our stories and epics as exemplifications of scientific or historical facts. The claims made by the chronicles of our past should not be tested either for their accuracy or for their 'truth'. Instead, as Indians, we learn to deal differently with our '*itihasa*', as we call our epics and puranas. Now we can appreciate the danger: in fighting for the 'truth' (or the factual nature) of Ramayana and Mahabharata, we would *root out* the attitudes towards *itihasa* that have been transmitted to us over the millennia. How can that happen?

Even though *we*, the current generation, might feel thrilled by the discovery that Kurukshetra is geographically localized in India, our children and grandchildren *will not*. To them, it will be a mere region in India in some Indian texts, which they would care to read either as 'poetry' or not at all. The words '*Dharmakshetre Kurukshetre*' will not and cannot find any resonance in them, even though they conjure up *to us* a complex world which we continue to be a part of even today. If we nevertheless persist in an endeavour to transform *itihasa* into historiography, perhaps parts would remain as 'facts' but most would disappear from the memories of our children and grandchildren. Then, it would destroy the ways the *mahakavyas* live on with people in India. *Bhaktas* of Rama and Hanuman would end up as urban legends or folktales and not living emergences of a culture, as is the case today. To the posterity, if this future comes to be, Rama and Lakshmana, among other things, would not any more remain as brothers to emulate, as they are to us, but only the names of some local princes from somewhere and somewhen. In short: making *itihasa* into history would destroy our past, because, as the world shows us today, *the best way to destroy the past of a people is to give them history.*

This is not the only danger portended by the process of transforming itihasa into facts about the past. *Stories are units of learning in a culture* that teaches through them. Making these into a conglomeration of facts would block a learning process that lends specificity to our culture.

The third aspect of the danger is that stories would become prescriptives dressed up in moral values, e.g.: Rama would become a weak Indian imitation of Jesus of Nazareth. If our itihasa simply outlines Western and Biblical morality, then we are destined to emerge as the vanquished: our puranas would become lurid stories about immoral gods and unethical heroes. Lines from Biblical commandments, 'thou shalt respect thy parents' and 'thou shalt not commit adultery', would then better summarize what Valmiki and Vyasa could not express adequately even in their big tomes. It comes down to this: when we attempt to transform our traditions into a variant of Semitic religions, we can only become its 'pale and erring variant'.

In short: we must note that neither deriding the absence of history writing in India nor its antipode that makes our itihasa into historical documents is useful to us. Both are born from colonialisms and are the results of a semi-total destruction of our native intellectual traditions. We are in urgent need of a new breed, that is, intellectuals rooted in Indian culture but 'at home' with Western intellectual riches. Creating them is the task for the future.

CHAPTER 2

SYMBOLICALLY INTERPRETING SHIVA?

About two decades ago, at an international conference in India, the participants held their plenary sessions in a reasonably large room. In the corner of the room, there were two big statues: one of a dancing Durga, and the other of a dancing Ganesha. In one of the plenary meetings, the last session if I remember correctly, a foreign delegate asked what these statues were and what they were doing. The organizer of the conference, an Indian woman, said they were statues of Durga and Ganesha. "What are they?" After some uncomfortable shuffling of feet, this woman (who got her Ph.D. in the US) said that they were 'aesthetic objects'. I got annoyed at that and stood up and explained to the other delegates that these statues were no art objects of any kind. I told them they were the representations of our *devatas* and asked the organizer the following question: since when do Indians find an elephant headed, fat-bellied clumsy dancer with multiple arms beautiful? Which Indian woman would marry a groom who looked like Ganesha and consider him beautiful? Since when is a naked dancing woman with eight arms that hold different objects, including a human skull dripping with blood, and with a tongue at least two feet long, considered to be an epitome of feminine beauty in India? Of course, one could say that these 'aesthetic' objects do not embody our notions of beauty but our ideas of ugliness instead and that these statues could themselves be beautiful 'art objects' despite expressing our notions of ugliness. In that case, we would still be at a loss to understand the affection, the devotion or even the fondness Indians show to these *devatas*. Indians do not talk about Durga or Ganesha in aesthetic terms, even when they find Baby Ganesha 'cute'.

Because this woman, and many like her, are embarrassed by the questions asked by foreigners, they transform us into aesthetic imbeciles: either our notion of beauty is embodied by ugly creatures, or the *devatas* 'worshipped' by Indians are as ugly as can be. Instead of telling stories about Durga and Ganesha and how we should understand them, this woman and others of her kind come up with symbolic interpretations that make us seem like cretins, and/ or force us into avenues that have us contrast the 'grotesque' forms in our temples with the paintings of Michelangelo representing the Divinity at the Sistine Chapel. At least partially, this has to do with our ignorance of the nature of stories and their roles in our culture.

A STANDARD STORY

Here is one standard way of looking at stories. They are symbols, it is said. Of what are they symbols? Well, they could symbolize acts – in the manner of Shiva's *Taandava* dance symbolizing Cosmic destruction. They could also be *symbolic justifications*. For instance, Rama's departure from Ayodhya expresses the filial obligation of a son to obey his father, no matter how foolish that father is. The stories could be seen to symbolize virtues like courage or vices like greed. One could see in them symbols of passion, feeling, natural forces… In all such cases, stories require that we *interpret* them.

If talking about a story, or telling one, involves interpretation, we need to note too that there are always multiple interpretations available in the marketplace. How do we decide which interpretation is better, and what happens when interpretations conflict? If our choices are based merely on our likes and preferences, they become dependent on our background or cultural beliefs, prejudices, or pet theories.

Here, 'interpretation' carries a literal meaning: some object from one domain (in our case, the domain of stories) is *interpreted* by mapping it onto an object from another domain (the domain of events, values, natural forces, actions, both human and divine…). It is not a logical or a mathematical function that does this mapping *but an interpreter and his subjectivity*. In that case, the disagreement between people becomes an issue of acceptability of interpretations. One finds an interpretation 'respectable' while another says it is 'indecent'; one is 'shocked' by an interpretation, while the other is comforted that it is 'conservative'; one rejects an interpretation because it is 'reactionary', whereas the other accepts it precisely because of its 'progressive' nature, and so on.

There is a dominant conception of myth in the Western intellectual tradition that contrasts myth with fact. The one is false (a myth), it is not history; the other is true (a fact), the building block of scientific historiography. We can stretch this stance and claim that rituals too are symbols that enact 'sacred' myths. Many, many Indians, and Indologists, both foreign and domestic, accept this notion and raise all kinds of questions. What do rituals mean? What do meditative *mudras* mean? Why perform funerary rites? How can a modern-day scientist perform rituals for his deceased parents or do Ganesha puja, when he goes to his science laboratory immediately thereafter? Do not these symbolic acts signify the superstition of such a scientist? The activity of answering these questions has provided a lucrative career for many over the last few centuries. There are innumerable 'facts' and 'interpretations' one can offer as answers to the above questions.

AN OPENING SALVO

Let me begin our journey by taking an example that I will return to much later in the book. This is not a fictitious example but one that recurs in textbooks and is encountered in many face-to-face conversations.

Person X: "In Ancient India, there existed a fertility cult that worshipped the Lingam, which symbolizes the phallus. That practice continues to this day, even though most Indians are ignorant of this symbolism. The repressed sexual attitude of the Indian male indexes the truth and strength of this symbolism."

To keep the contrast between me and person X stark, here is what I say: the *Lingam is not a symbol of anything or anybody*. The Lingam is *how* puja is done to Shiva by Indians, as contrasted to, say, how we do *puja* to Vishnu or Rama.

Now, person X tells me that the above *factual claim* is wrong. Very well. We must realize that I am stating a fact and not providing any interpretation, whereas *person X is*. He tells me that I do something *other than* Shiva puja, namely, I worship a 'symbol' that, in turn, belongs in a fertility cult. Consequently, *he* must justify his interpretation of my act.

Why does he think this way? Why does he think that our ancestors taught us to do *puja* to a symbol instead of saying outright that *puja* is done to the phallus, even if it meant admitting their obsession with Shiva's organ? Can we assume *their* obsession with the Lingam and that is why they zeroed in on Shiva – because of their 'prudishness' or their 'sexual repression'? (By the way, did you know the core reference of the word 'prude'? In Europe, one did not bathe in the nude because exposing or even looking at one's genital organs could *tempt a person to sin*. Therefore, people bathed while dressed in their underclothes. This practice persisted among faithful Christians till the end of the Second World War. Such a person, who bathes in his underclothes, is a 'prude'.) There is no evidence that this was also the case with our ancestors; my interlocutor merely assumes that they were sexually repressed.

Besides, if bare breasted women were sculpted on temple walls in India during that period, and our ancestors gave the world the *Kama Sutra*, why did they (a) first invent a symbol for the phallus, (b) then precisely deny this symbolism and (c) thereafter, cook up some utterly fantastic story about both? If modern-day Indians cooked up such a story, perhaps one could use X's story about 'sexual repression' to explain it. Yet, as he says, most Indians do not even *know* they are worshipping a symbol. Well, to me and to others, X must make this plausible: why did our ancestors ever take to symbolism and cook up fantastic stories to camouflage their 'true' meanings? Why take a devious route instead of simply saying that one worships the phallus irrespective of its form or size? Pouring some cheap Freudian sauce over third-rate anthropology does not answer these questions. Consider why.

Until person X comes up with explanations for this peculiar 'deviousness' of our ancestors, I am justified in saying this: we do what our ancestors did, i.e., we do *puja* to Shiva in the form of the *lingam*. Because this simple story does not satisfy person X and he requires the complicated talk of fertility cults and symbolisms, I am justified in remaining a sceptic until he comes up with a satisfactory explanation. Currently, he does not have it; nor do I believe that he ever will. You will immediately see that I am adopting a scientific and rational attitude here. When two explanations of the 'same' phenomenon exist, one chooses the simpler one instead of the more complicated. They call this 'Occam's razor'. In our case, this means that person X must account for our practices: why did our ancestors have a need to hide their worship of the phallus and seek symbolic explanations? How and why am I seduced into doing *puja* to the Shiva lingam because of sexual repression? Compared to this complicated and non-existent narrative, my account is simpler. I do *puja* to the Shiva lingam because that is how I was taught to do *puja* to Shiva. Furthermore, there is also a Puranic story about it. There is no symbolism or deviousness of any kind here. We can accept this simple account is better than a non-existent, complex narrative because of Occam's razor. This is also the standard scientific practice.

THE BEGINNING OF A JOURNEY

None of what is said above prevents us from asking, "why did our ancestors begin doing puja to the Shiva Lingam?" To this question, there are multiple answers: the first answer might give us the story of Shiva and his anger with the Rishis in a forest. This is but one *puranic* answer; other answers come from the multiple *sthalapuranas* that tell us stories about a specific temple and the *lingam* in that temple. One might be unhappy or dissatisfied with such stories and question their truth value. One might want to know whether these stories are true or false. Consider now the question: *Why should these stories be either true or false?*

To the ancient Greeks and Romans, the stories of Aphrodite, Venus, Zeus, Jupiter, etc., were not objects of truth claims; the predicates 'true' and 'false' were simply not applicable to the many stories about their deities. The stories were not about human beings and earthly events but about gods, the events in their divine world and their divine actions in our mundane world. Therefore, the predicates 'true' and 'false' are not applicable to them and many stories could co-exist without conflict, even if, from the outside, they appeared contradictory. Aristotle, whose definition of 'truth' is still accepted by us today (philosophers and linguists call it the 'Aristotelian' or 'Semantic' conception of truth), did not reject Greek epics as false *because* they made contradictory statements. Two contradictory statements cannot both be true at the same time, in the same way. Even though disagreements between bards were noticed by the ancient Greeks, and even though a thinker like Plato fulminated about the bards and the role their stories played in corrupting 'upright' young Athenians, there was no empirical reason to call such stories false. Because these stories were not about humans but the divinities instead, here one cannot use the predicates 'true' and 'false'. My point is not about the existence of divinities and whether their world also exists; but that such stories are not about humans and their world.

We can make true or false statements only about the human and the mundane. Because of *what these stories were not about,* the ancient Greeks and Romans did not look at their stories as true or false.

With the emergence and the victory of Christianity, a new dynamic manifested itself in the Ancient world. Christians thought of the Ancients as worshippers of demons. This English word comes from *daimones,* the Greek word indicating those 'lower gods' who did not live on Mount Olympus. This is something like our *'kshudra devatas'.* The father of these demons was Satan or the Devil himself. When the Church Fathers tried to show that the Greeks and the Romans had 'false religion', they did so by considering ancient stories as bearers of truth values. The Devil was the King of the Earth; his minions and lieutenants—the lesser *daimones*—obeyed and followed his command; the Greeks and the Romans worshipped these entities. Consequently, all their stories were false since the Devil is the Father of Lies, and the contradictions in their stories became apparent to all those who believed in the 'true religion' that Christianity was. Unlike the Bible, which was the Truth, Greek myths were false and contradictory. Of course, they never denied that there was nonsense, ambiguities, and contradictions to be found in the Bible as well. But they took to symbolisms and a 'hermeneutic' reading of the Bible to make it maximally consistent. Because God, the perfect being, could never be inconsistent and is always perfectly trustworthy, His word (the Bible) could not be anything less. It had to be perfectly consistent and completely true. However, the 'Apostolic tradition' was the requirement to read and understand the real message of the Bible. The 'faults' that one discovers in the Bible are the results of not knowing how to read the Bible and demonstrate the clear influence of the Devil on the believer. Thus, the Church Fathers did something that the Ancient thinkers (the discoverers of science) never attempted – scrutinize their epics for logical consistency, rhetorical coherence and evaluate them for their truth.

Like the Christians who shaped their thought, the Enlightenment philosophers failed to understand that the Roman and Greek stories were not doctrines to be believed as true or false or to be looked at as descriptions of the world. They ridiculed these 'mythologies'. Some saw them as fictionalized and embellished accounts of human history; some said they symbolically edified human virtues and passions; yet others found all these stories silly because they were nothing but superstitious expressions of primitive fears. Our erstwhile colonial masters, the British, were both the progenitors of and heirs to this tradition.

In contrast to these standard perspectives stands my conceptualization of stories. As I see the issue, stories are *exemplars*, namely entities addressing and solving problems of executing original and new actions in novel situations. They are not false; nor are they true (they are not facts). As *action heuristics*, i.e., as rules of thumb, they can be neither true nor false. Because of their nature, one and the same story can function in multiple contexts, with no 'moral rule' attached to it (the way it is with the fables of Aesop; after all, *Hitopadesha* is not itihasa). Stories that have this status as *modes of transmission of knowledge* are prized in a culture dominated by practical or performative knowledge. Not only do stories transmit; they could also guide the processes of discovery. Thus, as products of human imagination, they are on par with other products like poetry, literature, music, dance, philosophy, scientific theories.

However, to understand what stories are to a culture requires having a *theory* about cultural differences; such a theory would account for the ways in which, say, Indian culture differs from Western culture. Accounting for these differences will include, *inter alia*, such issues as the role of stories in that culture.

CHAPTER 3

WHAT IS CULTURE?

Afamous cemetery in the domain of anthropology is the definitions of 'culture'. There are more discredited and junked definitions of culture than anthropological theories. There is little point in rehearsing the problems faced by multiple definitions of this word. Instead, I want to focus on how I use the term and what I mean in this book. To get this idea across in a simple manner, let me sketch a simplified story.

Unlike most other species, humankind does not come well-equipped to survive birth unattended and uncared for in the multiple environments it is born into, for great lengths of time. The role of parents, especially the mother, is crucial in this regard. The parents and the community of the human child educate it in multiple ways and the child learns in equally diverse ways to survive and flourish. There are two environments basic to us: the natural environment and the social environment which mediates us to the former. Again, unlike other species, we are not programmed to learn in any specific way to survive in our environments. Whether our ability to learn a language is innate or not, it is indisputable that linguistic communication is crucial for our survival. Equally crucial is our ability to learn by modelling the actions of others, whether those others are our parents, siblings, friends, and so on. Thus, to put it in quite simple terms, learning a language and learning through modelling actions are important for us to live and flourish in the two complex environments in which we find ourselves.

Any group that survives as a culture would thus have built two extremely rich storehouses containing two things: linguistic items and actionable items. Even though this distinction appears simple, their diversity and complexity are enormous: human languages and human institutions are extraordinarily varied. The latter – whether family, marriage, rituals, child rearing, schools, clubs, legal and political organizations – are congealed human actions. Poems, stories, theories, hypotheses, speeches, and talks are embodied in languages. As we grow up, our elders draw upon these multiple storehouses to educate us. Through education, we learn to make our environments habitable, i.e., learning is a way of creating a habitat. As we learn, we also draw upon the treasure chests that our teachers use.

Not only do we draw upon these resources, but we also learn *how to use them* both to learn and to go about with things in our two environments. The same consideration applies to those who teach us. They too use this reservoir of knowledge to teach us to use it better. Because these resources used by both teachers and their pupils help us to relate to others, we could call them the '*resources of socialization*'.

In simple terms: human beings are socialized using the resources of socialization. As I indicated earlier, in this process, we also learn *how* to use these different resources. In the broadest terms, this is what a 'culture' is: the available resources for socialization and their uses. Cultural differences, thus, would reside in *how these resources are utilized or used* and in the identification of these resources. The different ways and manners in which individuals use resources of socialization would form the cultural person ('culturality') the way the psychology of an individual forms the psychological person ('personality') and the sociology of an individual forms his social person ('sociality'). As I once put it: "What makes a difference, any difference, into *cultural* difference and not social, psychological or biological difference? Some difference (between individuals) is a cultural difference if it *entails a specific way of using the resources of socialization.*"

This simple outline is enough for us to speak about cultural differences between India and, say, the West. The difference between the two does not lie merely in the difference in content between the items of socialization but, more importantly, in *how* they use this content. In the modern-day world, more items of socialization are common (or shared) between cultures: from schools through political institutions to our discussions about these. The differences in content between the British and Indian parliaments and their structural similarity help us understand the political differences and similarities between the two. However, their *cultural* difference is indexed by how these institutions are used in society: from how the legislators act (both in and outside the parliament) to how individuals relate to them. How children are brought up, how child-rearing takes place in India culturally differentiates India from the UK, even where the same institutions (family, day care centres, schools, etc.) are used and the children are taught in, say, English. An account of cultural differences tracks such differences.

How do these cultural differences come into existence, how are they reproduced and transmitted across generations? My hypothesis to account for this, in a simplified form again, is the following: the learning processes that create the different resources of socialization are themselves diverse. These processes are coordinated and made into a configuration, which I call a '*configuration of learning*'. Cultures are produced and reproduced by these configurations of learning and the differences between such configurations are what we call cultural differences. (I cannot go into detail here, those who are interested can see Chapter 1 of *Reconceptualizing India Studies*, 2012)

Quite obviously, these configurations of learning have origins. Some or the other thing coordinates the multiple learning processes present in human groups into a configuration. My hypothesis is that religion creates a configuration that brings forth Western culture; and it is ritual that plays this role in producing Indian culture.

This is enough for our present purposes. When I speak of differences between Indian and Western cultures, I have these two different configurations of learning in mind. The cultural difference between an Indian and a Westerner would lie in how they use the resources of socialization available to them and this use is determined by how they have learnt (and have been taught) to use them. Both the learner and the teacher are guided here by their configurations of learning. These ideas are necessary to make clear that I *do not* plot cultural differences along geographical, or linguistic or religious lines. Thus, belonging to Indian culture is how we use or deal with the resources of socialization in India. This would mean that belonging to this or that religion does *not* differentiate people as members of a culture: one could belong to Indian culture whether a Jain, Buddhist or a Hindu in exactly the same way a Christian or a Muslim is Indian. This accords with what we see in India: a Konkani-speaking Muslim in Mumbai is as much an Indian as a Kannada-speaking Christian in Mangalore, and as a Tamil-speaking Brahmin in Bangalore. This statement and the sentiment it expresses are only superficially puzzling. The puzzle is how it is possible to put the colonizers (the Muslims and Christians) at the same level as the colonized (a Mylapore Brahmin). Let me remind you that I said in the beginning that we were colonized by Islam and the British. We must keep this in mind: Islam colonized us but not Muslims; the British colonized us but not their Christianity. A religion (Islam) and a people (the British) were our colonizers. The British left a very small part of their people behind: the Anglo-Indians, whose particular 'interests' are protected even to this day in and by our parliament. Their hyphenated identity leaves no doubt that they are Indians too, even if not in the same way an Indian Muslim is that without the hyphenation. The Jews, the Muslims or the Christians are not hyphenated in India and it is about them that I speak.

However, there is also a second puzzle: I suggested above that religion produces and reproduces a *configuration*. In that case, how do we understand the role of Christianity and Islam in India? Are not the followers of these religions socialized differently because of their religion, and is not their presence a disturbing factor for Indian culture? Why would these religions not produce their configurations of learning and adapt instead to the Indian configuration of learning? My answer will be simplified here again: when these religions entered India, they met a culture that was already formed as a stable configuration of learning. As a result, these religions had to adapt themselves to this culture to survive. That is, these religions could continue to hold their beliefs and practice their religious activities only by adapting to Indian uses of the resources of socialization. Thus, Indian Christianity and Indian Islam remain Indian irrespective of their religious beliefs and practices. The specificities of their religions are given a space to survive and flourish in Indian culture as one of the many diversities present within it. In this process, these religions themselves undergo modifications and changes in how the believers live their daily life, which does not affect their beliefs (say about Christ or Mohammed) or their places of worship. It is this kind of adoption of and adaptation into Indian culture that many Madrassa schools fight. It is this adaptation to India that Catholicism and Protestantism in India have undergone which the Evangelical Christians militate against. Whether such resistance has any effect at all or not depends not on their militancy but on the vibrancy of Indian culture. A vibrant Indian culture (because it is a culture) allows a place for these religions and absorbs their drive to create other configurations of learning within its own multiplicities that constitute a configuration of learning. These religions, on their own, cannot do what the military, economic and administrative powers that supported them, viz., colonialism, could not do, which is to destroy Indian culture. However, this does not mean that the two colonialisms did not damage Indian culture. They did, and their effects are still visible. We will discover what these are in later chapters.

In any case, you need to keep in mind that when I speak of 'Indian culture', I use the word differently than some associations we commonly make. As noticed, I do not identify culture either with regions, or languages or religions, but rather as configurations of learning. Now the question is this: why accept my hypotheses? How to begin evaluating my proposal? These are legitimate and reasonable questions to ask. In the process of answering them, I can also focus sharply on the theme of this book: what does it mean to be 'Indian'?

One of the crucial tests for evaluating claims about any culture, including Indian culture, is the extent to which such claims can make *sense* of the experiences of people *without denying, distorting, or preventing access* to such experiences. To use my favourite example: theories – in our case theories about Indian culture – must be capable of doing what Galileo's theory did. They must show us *why* we experience the world the way we do. They should not tell us that we hallucinate or have false *experiences* ("Your experience of Shiva puja is false" or "you are hallucinating if you think you are doing puja"); instead, they must show us *why* we experience the world the way we do. X cannot explain our experiences if all he can say is that I am primitive or that my absurd beliefs guide my irrational behaviours. Such a sentence is neither an explanation nor a theory. And we need both in my case. A single or even a couple of sentences are not 'theories'. When doing science and developing hypotheses about any kind of phenomena, we put very strong and robust conditions on what counts as a theory and what can be called an explanation although American television pundits jump up and down berating and crying about conspiracy 'theories'.

We do not hallucinate when we see the sun moving across the horizon; nor do we lie when we speak of the sunrise and sunset. In the same way, I do not hallucinate or lie when I say that I do *puja* to the Shiva lingam. I cannot be expressing any kind of neurosis in these cases, unless a theory comes up and proves that I have a neurosis that generates the beliefs and behaviours I have about Shiva, Shiva lingam and *puja*.

Thus, we need to better understand what this 'experience' is, which person X denies and distorts. I will tackle this issue in its generality first.

PART I

TO BE RAISED IN A CULTURE...

CHAPTER 4

EXPERIENCE AND ANUBHAVA: I

Let me begin by assuming that you would not disagree if I said that theories about the cultural worlds have their roots in the experiences of such worlds. By reflecting on experiences and describing them, theories help us think through issues and questions. Thus, if I want to theorize about Indian culture, I require access to an experience of Indian culture, whether directly or indirectly.

In chapter 2, we saw that thinking of the Lingam as a fertility symbol generates a sense of 'wrongness' in us. Why? Because our experience of Shiva *puja* is at odds with this explanation. At odds in which way? What X must explain becomes different from what he thinks he has explained. He must explain why I do puja to Shiva Lingam. But what he does is to postulate or assume a connection between a neurosis that I am supposed to be suffering from and the actions that I call puja. He assumes too that these actions are cultic practices. Cults, you must know, are degenerate small versions of 'religions'. Because all decent and righteous people worship God, the only entity that is truly worthy of worship, the respectable and respected 'religion' is contrasted with disreputable entities like 'cults'. (For instance, this is how the practices of Greeks and Romans were described by Christianity.) Thus, I am alleged to indulge in a base action (the Devil's worship, for instance) like a cultic practice. This too belongs to the collection of words Indians use without knowing their meaning along with 'sects' and 'mythology'. But more on this later.

According to X: the object of my action is a phallic shaped stone which indicates that I am expressing a repressed sexual instinct. In performing this action, I exhibit a neurosis. X refers to a Viennese gentleman called Freud in support. In this explanation, which is as pseudo as they come, where is Shiva, the Shiva Lingam or puja? They are absent. If they are absent from an alleged explanation, how could X be explaining what I experience or what I do? X does not answer this question at all; he simply assumes that my practice is cultic and that I am an idiot and a neurotic. Thus, even though our experience is that we do puja to Shiva, the explanation is neither about the puja nor about Shiva.

It is possible that I am a neurotic and an unhealthy person; it is also possible that my sexual instincts are repressed. However, when the explanation says further that I have false experiences, it is mouthing nonsense.

This is not an unknown phenomenon; let me formulate it here as an error: people often *confuse an explanation of experience with the experience itself.* Consequently, when you reject an explanation of an experience, they mistakenly think you deny the experience itself. If the sun does not revolve around earth (the geocentric explanation says it does), that does not imply that our experience of the sun's apparent movement is false or wrong. If we deny the existence of the Indian caste system or deny its causal role in explaining oppression in India, it does not mean we deny the existence of *jatis* or of any oppression that exists in Indian society. If I deny that the conflict between Muslims and Hindus is a 'religious conflict', I do not deny that conflict exists and has existed between Muslims and Hindus, or other non-Muslim groups, in India. In all such cases, I am merely rejecting an explanation of the experience without denying the experience itself.

Many people are ignorant of this fundamental distinction between 'having an experience' and 'having an explanation for experience'.

Ordinary folk might be oblivious about this distinction. But how about extra-ordinary folk like scientists and philosophers? Why do they commit the same mistake with almost the same frequency? What makes it difficult for them to keep this distinction in mind? Or, more generally put: where does this error come from? Why does it persist? What is the nature of the ignorance of this distinction that makes us forget that the distinction even exists? Why does learning about this distinction not eliminate it forever from the republic of knowledge? I will return to these questions later, but first let us look at the difference between experience and its explanation a bit more in detail.

When I see a see a mirage in a desert, the explanations of this phenomenon in optics and physics *do not deny that I see a mirage.* Science does not say that I hallucinate and explain that away by postulating a possible handicap or disorder. On the contrary. Its theories tell me that I must necessarily see a mirage and explain this experience by saying that it is a phenomenon in the world related to heat and refraction of light, because of which an oasis or water source is perceived. Scientific explanations do not deny what we see, observe or experience: (a) they explain what we experience, observe or see as existing in the world; and (b) if the perceived phenomenon does not exist, they provide an explanation that tells us why we *necessarily* must experience it anyway.

Science saves phenomena without denying them. Person X, on the other hand, gives me an explanation that not only does not save the phenomenon but also denies my experience. It says that I cannot possibly experience what I claim to be doing (puja to Shiva) because what exists in the world is another phenomenon altogether (neurosis). Even if we assume that the phenomenon described by person X does exist, its mere existence is not evidence for the claim that some other phenomenon cannot exist. Even if Shiva Lingam is a symbol of a fertility cult, that fact alone cannot deny that I do puja and I see the Shiva Lingam. Thus, his explanation is at loggerheads with my experience. Whatever else he 'explains', he is not explaining either puja or my doing it to the Shiva Lingam.

To think about 'Indian experience', we must speak of experiences that make them 'Indian' – in our example, it involves doing puja to the Shiva Lingam. But the explanations that we routinely reproduce, namely, those that appeal to fertility cults, symbolisms and sexual repressions, hint that there is no such thing as an 'Indian experience' because Indian culture is not 'monolithic', unless we indicate Indian 'hallucinations' (in the plural, nota bene) when we use that phrase. Some philosophically oriented spirits might even tell us that to speak of 'Indian experience' is to hypostatize abstract concepts like 'nation' or to reify processes like 'experience' into objects and substances. The result? Feeling a sense of 'wrongness' but not knowing how to reply, we simply fall silent, our lips stitched tightly together, dumb as human beings can ever be. This is no tearjerker, but the lot and daily life of cultures of colonized peoples.

ACCESSING EXPERIENCE TODAY

Indian traditions, without exception as far as I know, have made experience and its interrogation central to their enquiry. Naturally, they too discovered that experience is not always reliable and that there are difficulties in accessing our experience. "I keep on making the same mistake over and over again despite many experiences", as we say many times. Indian traditions name such difficulties differently: *Maaya, Avidya,* and *Agyaana,* are some of the best-known categories in this context. Some call such difficulties as instances of *'paapa'* and, in fact, removing it has been one of the central goals:

Gyaanodaya or the 'arising of knowledge' (again, called differently by different traditions) is said to remove paapa or these difficulties or impediments. These hindrances are either 'illusions' of some kind, or ignorance of some kind. We can remove them, these traditions tell us, and they developed multiple ways of doing so. In fact, the plurality of the Indian traditions partly expresses the fact that there is a plurality of ways of removing ignorance. Though ill-understood by most Indologists and philosophers, these ideas are important. Ignorance does not just connote 'absence of information'; it also refers to a 'force' that plays an active role in hindering the process through which knowledge emerges.

Let us understand what it means to access the Indian traditions and our experiences. When we say we access the Indian traditions, we indicate two things: (a) it is possible for us to access them; (b) we know *how* to access them. That is, to grow up within the framework of the Indian traditions does not merely mean that we have the possibility of accessing these traditions if we want to, but it also means that we have learnt how to access them as and when we want. For the sake of convenience, we can put it this way: *in ideal conditions*, when brought up in Indian culture, we learn two things: (a) we learn to access our traditions (one ability); (b) we also learn a specific way of accessing them (another ability). If we use the knowledge produced by the earlier generations, i.e., if we understand how they accessed experiences of their world, we can learn their way. Thus, *the second ability, learning from the earlier generations, helps us access our traditions and our experiences of today*. If we learn only to access our traditions, depending on how the first ability is transmitted, we might have to reinvent the wheel by the cumbersome process of trial and error, stumbling and standing upright, going through dead ends and false avenues, to learn the second ability – a specific way to access. Some might succeed in this venture, where others fail. There are no signposts, no heuristics, and no established results to work with. In the ideal conditions that I am talking about, we also learn 'the Indian way' of accessing. Thus, the second ability is also transmitted to us in our culture. In such an ideal case, both abilities are transmitted; in a worst-case scenario, a culture disintegrates because neither of the two abilities is transmitted.

This brings me to the point where I can explicitly formulate what I mean by 'Indian culture'. It is a culture where knowledge is mainly experiential in nature – it is practical knowledge that is a means to form and reflect upon experience. This knowledge makes sense when rooted in experience; it is about experience; its goal is to shape and transform human experience. Indian theories are about experiences and were devised to think about how to change them.

ON ANUBHAVA

We undergo many events and happenings; we encounter many objects and events; we have varied and multiple relations with people and animals; we see, taste, smell, hear, and touch many objects both natural (fruits, flowers, vegetables, bird calls) and manmade (incense, ice-cream, wine, music). We react, feel, think, walk, run... Here, I speak generically and say, 'we undergo events, persons, objects, etc., in the world'. More simply, we undergo things in the world. These are the *raw materials* for *constructing* experiences.

These raw materials are *transformed* into experiences. This extremely complex process is not only learnt but also continuously relearnt by us. In this learning, we slice what we encounter into manageable fragments and give them structure. That is, the transformation consists of *structuring* what we undergo.

We can talk about '*experience*' only if the transformation is successful. If the transformation is a failure, then we have '*trauma*'. Even though we talk about 'experiencing a trauma', we undergo a trauma. A trauma is the retention of what we undergo in the world in a partially unstructured manner. It is only partially structured because this *structuring* mostly names what we have undergone. However, it does not belong to the set of experiences that are structured. Because it remains only as 'that which we have undergone', we undergo (re-live) it again and again (mentally when the physical event is in the past) and suffer. The suffering is double: (a) it remains unstructured because of which it continuously returns as though we undergo it regularly; and (b) partly because of this, it does not become a mere memory. To use an analogy, it is like pain that refuses to become a memory: remembering having pain is different from undergoing that pain. That is, having the pain of your teeth being pulled without an anaesthetic is different in kind from remembering that it was painful when your teeth got pulled without an anaesthetic. Trauma re-lives the pain long after an event is over, not by remembering it but by remaining unstructured and by being named or identified as 'something horrible'. You undergo the event repeatedly and this trauma disappears only when it is structured and becomes an experience.

How do we structure what we undergo? We use the 'resources of socialization' that are available in our culture. What are they? The variety is great: family life, friends and peer groups, formal and informal education, civil institutions and organizations like schools, trades unions, political parties, media, etc. They also include stories, rituals, lore, legends, poetry and so on. These resources teach us not only how to go about with events, objects and happenings but also with thoughts, feelings, perceptions, etc. A culture also teaches its members the use of these resources. That is, cultures teach not only which resources to use but also how to use them. Using these resources, we structure what we undergo in the world into experiences.

Different cultures teach us to structure what we undergo in different ways. Stories, for instance, play an important role in transforming what we undergo, and different stories do it in different ways. Whether it is about how to do puja, or about ideas of friendship or how to think about ourselves, the way we experience these are determined by what our culture teaches us and how what we undergo is structured. What I have said so far can be summarized in a simple form: experiences are structured, and we learn how to do that from our culture. In a non-trivial sense, our experiences are cultural in a deep sense of the word 'cultural'.

You can understand some of the above ideas better, if we look at 'Anubhava', which is how we translate the English word 'experience'. Two words in Sanskrit and in many other Indian languages are compounded here; in Sanskrit, they are the pre-fix *Anu* and the root *Bhu*. Anu has multiple meanings, including 'similar', 'to imitate', 'to follow', and we can be render it here as 'apt' or 'appropriate'. The root word Bhu means 'to be', indicating 'being'. Thus, Bhava is translated as 'being' or 'existence'. (*Anubhava*, which translates 'experience', also indicates one of the sources of knowledge.) We could say that the word indicates an appropriate existence; or that there is an appropriate way of being-in-the-world. *Appropriate to what*, though? Appropriate to things, events, actions, and people that we encounter.

To have anubhava, then, is to be appropriately present in our encounters. It is being-present-with. To do this, mostly we need time: to relate appropriately to different things in the world. We must take our time and get to know these things if we are to relate appropriately to them. If one wants anubhava, one must take the time, have patience, be there and get to know. In short, anubhava indicates how we deal with what we encounter – when we think, taste, perceive, hear, feel, touch. In this sense, it is also about learning to deal with sensations, perceptions, feelings, and thoughts. To do this, we use the resources available to us; we learn to use the resources of socialization to shape, transform and structure what we undergo in the world into an anubhava or an experience. From now on, I will use anubhava and experience interchangeably.

This idea suggests that we must learn *how* to experience. We need learning because we are not genetically programmed to have experiences. We must stay receptive, be open to the world and wait upon things, events, and people. Note, however, that neither the receptivity nor the 'waiting upon' is passive: we must learn to be rightly receptive and appropriately wait upon people ('anu'). And, of course, we must also think. Thus, *learning to be a human being is also to learn to experience.*

In *one sense*, because experience has many elements, higher biological organisms (not just human beings) too can be said to have experience. After all such organisms too undergo processes and events in the world and deal with what they encounter. In this sense, you cannot decide whether to have or not to have experiences. How can a human being decide or not decide to have thoughts or feel hot coal? Of course, we might choose not to have this or that specific experience (of drinking whisky, of going to the US and such like) but this is not identical to not having experience as such.

Yet, in the *second sense*, we also say that some people either have 'little' experience or do not learn from their experience or are traumatized by their experience. This arises from the fact that what has evolved through our encounter in the world might not be the most appropriate or adequate way of dealing with it. You might have learnt to get along with things you routinely encounter in the world, and you might think it adequate. You might even consider it *appropriate*. But appropriateness depends not only on your ability to cope with things but also with the nature of things you encounter. That is, the appropriateness that we talk about incorporates two dimensions: (a) the subjective dimension that refers to what you consider appropriate; (b) the objective dimension that picks out the fact that the world is also objective in nature: it is your world only because it is 'the world' as well.

Thus, you are compelled to *think*. You can modify, channelize, shape and fine-tune experience in such a way that you develop an appropriate way of being-in-the-world. Of course, this learning process requires teaching. The more you reflect about experience, the more you shape it by thinking about how you relate to the world, to its raw materials, its objects, events, happenings, creatures, thoughts, sensations, etc., and the nature of what you encounter. It is therefore an active process.

The more you do this, the more progress you make. Is there some way of indicating, if not exactly measuring, this progress? Is there a signpost of some sort? Indian traditions answer these questions in the affirmative: yes, there is. At a 'lower' stage, there is a sense of contentment and a sense of equilibrium. This is one way of knowing whether you are on the route to developing an appropriate way of being in the world. Over a period, both the frequency and duration of periods of internal equilibrium increase. The higher stage of experience is called *Ananda*. Some Indian traditions relate it very closely to anubhava by naming the higher stage *anu-bhaava*, i.e., a *bhaava* that is also *anu*. It is also termed Gyaanodaya or, the Indian notion of enlightenment. I will not go into this any further here.

CHAPTER 5

EXPERIENCE AND ANUBHAVA: II

We can now understand better what having a rich or a complex experience means. It says that you have structured what you have undergone in many rich and complex ways. We understand too why we can learn through experience and how it could be a source of knowledge: not only do we acquire abilities for dealing with the many things that we encounter in the world, but we also come to 'know' the world. Thus, experience teaches us about ourselves and the world. A terminus to experience is impossible because it involves learning by living-in-the-world. Your experience ends only when you cease to live-in-the-world.

Having an appropriate existence-in-the-world is one way of 'being in this world'. But you should not think that it is identical to performing a morally correct action or to having a right opinion on this or that subject. Some or another attitude you may have towards, say, abortion or universal franchise, is not a way of 'being' in the world.

Any creature dealing with things in the world has 'an appropriate existence' or experience. Here, 'dealing with' does not involve deliberate action. When you feel sorrow, you cry and that is how you deal with sorrow; you remove your hand hurriedly when it comes near burning coal and this is how you deal with its heat. You might say that crying and removing your hand are physical actions. But you also deal with sensations, etc. without performing any physical action. You may do nothing when you get angry or keep the sweets in your mouth longer to savour their taste or listen to music without doing anything. You undergo things, you respond. These too deal with emotions, sensations, etc. In this sense, one does not have to think about the world or act consciously just to 'experience'. Let us go through these steps in a slightly different way now and outline them a bit differently.

LEARNING TO DEAL WITH THE SENSES

Let us retain the translation of Anu as 'appropriate' or 'apt' but now emphasize the active dimension of the word Bhava by translating it as 'coming into existence'. Anubhava would then mean an apt way of coming-into-existence. But, *coming into existence of what?* Let us say: the coming-into-existence-of-being. We can shorten it as coming-into-being, i.e., we come into existence from somewhere else. Thus, we can say that bhava can be translated as being-there-in the world or as being-present-in-the-world. As we have seen, anubhava means 'being appropriately present in the world' or 'being aptly present in the world'. The 'anu', as it is used in the above formulation, does not use a standard to judge what is apt or appropriate.

Earlier, I said that all creatures, especially those with highly evolved nervous systems, can be said to have experience. While this draws our attention to what unites us with other creatures, switching our attention to emphasize the active dimension of bhava helps us see differences. Bhava can also mean *becoming*. Anubhava, in a less generic sense, is an apt becoming. *Becoming what?* Whatever. That is, using this word, we emphasize the process(es) of becoming, quite independent of what a creature becomes. To become (whatever you become), you must perdure or persist (in time) through the process of becoming. By undergoing this process, you go through a transition from one state to another, i.e., you undergo a state-change. The emphasis of anubhava is on transition here. So, to become human, you go through an 'apt' process of transition. Such transitions also involve learning.

If you must go through a state-change that also involves learning, a danger looms large: *things could interfere in this process in different ways*. These are the filters. They could prevent an apt state-change and hinder processes of learning. When they do so, we can justifiably speak about *not having access to our experience*. Colonialism introduced filters that hinder an apt state-change and block the learning that enables us to initiate such a process. These filters were introduced through violence and, as I have said elsewhere, they inflict violence on human beings in their effects too.

Functioning in the background is a vague idea: it is unclear what it is to be a human being, but the word anubhava indicates here that, in so far as a process of learning is involved, you become a human being in a preferred way. For the time being, let us say that anubhava involves going through a learning process that allows us to *aptly deal* with sounds, tastes, thoughts, feelings, and the senses associated with them. Which is the apt way? Every way is apt if it allows you to deal with your senses. Anubhava now suggests to us that it means *learning* to deal with our senses, no matter how we do that. The two colonialisms that we have undergone have introduced filters that *hinder this learning* violently. These filters prevent transition to an apt state. Nevertheless, in so far as every state is an apt state, there is transition. In a sense, the colonialisms cripple us by deforming experiences. But a crippled experience is still experience, even if crippled, and a crippled human being remains a human being.

The two colonialisms bring these together: *the crippled experience and the crippled human being become the norm and the normal.* A cripple who is born into a community of cripples and knows only of people crippled like him will assume that his state is the natural and normal state of being. He would also resist suggestions that he is not normal and is crippled. A thought experiment might help here. Would you be willing to accept that you are handicapped because your sense of sight, sound, and smell is limited, when compared to some animals and insects in this world? Or would you say that your so-called limitations make you human and differentiate you from other creatures? This is where we Indians are today.

We learn to deal with senses aptly: apt in so far as we deal with these senses 'rightly' and apt in so far as our senses also respond 'rightly' to the world. These are the subjective and the objective senses of the term aptness or appropriateness. This is not an individual learning process alone but one that requires and presupposes the existence of human communities. Depending upon their understanding of human beings, society, and the world, these communities will have generated multiple standards of aptness. For example, anger makes you keep quiet, makes you shout, scold, and so on; even these vary depending upon whether you are a child or an adult; and, even then, on who is present with you and so on. This is how you learn to deal with anger, for instance. The greater the variety of ways of dealing with your senses, the more you have learnt and the greater is your anubhava or experience.

Where does thinking about or reflecting on experience fit in this scheme? Through the process of thinking and experimenting, you refine the ways of dealing with the raw material of your anubhava or experience. They are more apt or become more appropriate as you go through life. The more anu they are, the more does your bhava change. You use an earlier anubhava to transform the subsequent ones: experience helps further refine experience. The repertoire of feelings and the ways of dealing with them grow and become more refined. We actively keep this in mind when we raise children:

we teach them that something is not simply 'anger' but that it is distinguishable from irritation or annoyance. *The richer a culture and its language, the more refined are its distinctions.* In Indian culture, we make hair-fine distinctions between emotions and behaviour. For example, in Kannada, 'konku' is different from 'kuhuka', which is not really 'akshepane' or even 'akeshpa' and yet is not 'vyangya' and is something other than 'huluku hudukodu'.

IS 'EXPERIENCE' THE SAME AS 'ANUBHAVA'?

Until now, I used 'experience' to translate 'anubhava'. Let us briefly look at possible differences in meaning between these two terms as well.

If we take English language-use as a reference, it appears as though we speak sensibly about experiencing our feelings ("I experience sadness"), experiencing thoughts ("I can even now experience my jumbled thoughts when..."), experiencing colour ("I experience a redness"), experiencing actions ("I still experience my shaking limbs when I...") and so on. That is, we experience *inputs* from our senses. From this, it follows that experience cannot be identical to any one of them. The elements of experience contain inputs from the sense organs in the form of thoughts, feelings, sensations, but experience *cannot be coextensive with any one of them.*

Let us look very briefly at the English word 'experience' which is used to translate anubhava. In Latin, the word *experientia* plays the role of the English word, which is derived both from the Latin root and medieval French. In its earlier uses, the word indicated a source of knowledge that enabled trials, experimentation, and the consequent acquisition of skills. In this use, we can see the connections between anubhava and experience. However, the core meaning of this word has begun to shift, best expressed in some Germanic languages, especially in German and Dutch. '*Erfahrung*' and '*ervaring*' (in

German and Dutch respectively) connote experience. Both have 'travel', 'journeying' ('to fare', in English) as core meanings: '*er-fahren*', '*er-varen*', indicating 'to go there'. This idea of 'journeying' suggests that these words emphasize the new, the novel, the strange and the unfamiliar as their components. In English too, this shift is noticeable: "It was such an experience to go up the Eiffel Tower"; "I had never experienced something like that before"; "Visiting the US or travelling in Europe is quite an experience"; "Listening to that concert or sitting in that cricket stadium is an experience in itself", and so on. In this process, the English word 'experience' has begun to drift away from the 'known' and the 'familiar' (after all, experimenting with or doing trials with something makes that thing familiar) to the unfamiliar, and from the familiar into the strange and alien. To interact in a novel situation or with a strange object is closer to the current usage of the word than dealing with the known and the familiar. The Indian word anubhava, by contrast, focusses on the familiar; on knowing it, on dealing with it aptly. If this drift in English continues, we will soon be unable to use anubhava to translate 'experience'. The first would focus on the familiar and the second on the unfamiliar and the strange. One use indicates that going about with the familiar is required for anubhava; the other would indicate that an encounter with the unfamiliar is required for experience.

In any case, if anubhava is to translate 'experience', it involves 'an awareness of a state-of-being-in-the-world'. This is not a definition but a mere circumscription of 'experience'. Let me use this circumscription to briefly look at the idea that experience is a source of knowledge. Even here, the focus will be on ignorance, the antonym of knowledge. The question is simple: *what is the source of ignorance?*

This is an important question because, at first sight, it looks as though ignorance does not and cannot have a source — if it is understood as an 'absence', namely, as absence of knowledge or information. The errors and mistakes we attribute to ignorance do not suggest that something absent in the world works as a cause to bring about some situation. Something must exist in the world if it is to be causally effective. What we mostly do in such cases is to attribute a causal role to false beliefs: because someone falsely believed that something was the case when it was not, he acted in the manner he did. ("I acted the wrong way, I realize now, because I believed, falsely, that some behaviour was permitted or correct.") If we look at it this way, errors and mistakes have their source or their origin in the falsity of beliefs: truth helps us act aptly while falsity leads us to errors and mistakes. In that case, ignorance is not the absence of knowledge alone but the presence of falsehood (disinformation). As we notice in this situation, knowledge is subordinated to truth. Truth is more important than knowledge. Because truth and falsehood divide the world of statements into two exhaustive partitions, falsehood and lies must be present where truth is absent.

Indians take a slightly different route because they privilege knowledge above truth. While knowledge is always true (there can be no false knowledge), not everything that is true is also knowledge. For instance, a telephone directory consists only of true statements, but we would not call it an exemplar of knowledge. Therefore, our thinkers said that there are two kinds of ignorance: (a) there is the kind of ignorance that signifies the absence of knowledge; (b) then there is the kind of ignorance which *actively* prevents the emergence of knowledge in human beings. There is also a third kind, which is a harmless variety of the second kind: (c) this kind indicates a situation where we have false beliefs, which we discard when faced with an alternative set of true beliefs. Important to note though is that the second kind of ignorance acts causally by hindering the emergence of knowledge. For now, think of it merely as a 'filter' that prevents a state-change in human organisms. It is a filter that hinders learning.

In this sense, it is active. What kind of a filter is it? In principle, it could be of any kind. Could truth – a true statement or a fact – hinder learning and prevent the emergence of knowledge? The surprising answer is: Yes. Often, human errors and mistakes are attributable to true facts and true statements. However, it is knowledge (which is always true) that liberates, not truth. The Good Book says that 'Truth liberates'. Indians do not assent to this: *truth can enslave, and only knowledge liberates.*

Ignorance, thus, prevents access to experience. Often, it is called '*maaya*'. However, it is not maaya alone that prevents access to our experience: our culture, our society, our individual psychology could also act as constraints in accessing our experience. If these are external factors, colonialism induced an additional hindrance to the process by creating more impediments. It took away our way(s) of accessing experience, leaving almost a vacuum in its place. This vacuum, in our case, has been filled by the adoption of a particular way of looking at Indian culture and her texts – a way we have learnt from the British. Thus, you and I face two impediments: the first is the vacuum created by one colonialism; the second is how the other colonialism filled that vacuum. These two further prevent access to our experience alongside other impediments like maaya.

Thus, to understand Indian people today, we must (1) understand the structure of human psychology, (2) the cultural psychology of Indians, (3) the historical impacts of different colonialisms, and so on.

CHAPTER 6

INTROSPECTING EXPERIENCE

Let us apply the results of the previous chapters to a common problem and look at what it means *to access and think* about experience. I will look not so much at what these words mean as much as what is entailed by (or what happens when we indulge in) the activity of thinking. During this attempt, a few things that might have sounded abstract to you in the previous chapter(s) will become tangible and concrete.

The best way to begin this analysis is by asking the following two questions about a familiar activity: what exactly do we do when we think about ourselves? Is there a 'right' way to think about ourselves? Let me begin with the first question. Because most of us often think about ourselves, I will take a rather trivial example and avoid complicated explanations and analyses.

Let us suppose that I lose my temper rather quickly – which happens to be true, by the way. This makes me say words I regret later and makes me wish I had spoken differently. Repetitive experiences of such situations make me want to control my temper or at least be able to control my tongue when I lose my temper. However, my experience is that I fail in doing either of the two. Infinite numbers of self-admonitions do not help; endless numbers of promises ("I shall not speak when I'm angry", or "I shall not get angry") fail to work. They only result in remorse, generate self-directed anger, and increase my sense of helplessness. There is a lot at stake here: fights, hurting people needlessly, messing up relationships and so on. Yet nothing, not even a study of books on psychology ever helps; my sense of helpless rage only keeps on getting fed.

Not many options are open to me. Either I hope for some miracle medication to control anger or I go to a psychologist and undergo psychoanalysis or some other therapy. The first is not available yet and, for many reasons, I prefer not to take the second option. Evolutionary biology tells me that this anger is the 'animal' part in me and that it is the result of too much production of some chemical in the brain or the misfiring of neural synapses. Even if this trait turns out to have a 'survival value' to my species, as evolutionary psychologists might want to put it, it is basically a handicap as far as I am concerned. So, I must live with it, but that precisely is the problem. I cannot and do not want to continue to live with my short temper. Yet, there do not appear to be too many options open to me. Not continuing to live with it, namely, committing suicide, is not much of an alternative in this context.

So, I seek help by thinking deeply about myself and talking to others, friends and wise people, about this problem of mine. None of this seems to help. If I think about myself, which includes detailed analyses of the situations where I lose my temper, and its alleged causes ("they insulted me"; "he was very rude"; "her accusations were unfounded"), it either makes me utterly despondent or ends up making me feel even more guilty. Sage advice from friends, like counting till ten before speaking, is impracticable. If I had the presence of mind to 'count till ten' when angry, I would also have the presence of mind to not say the nasty things I say. The fact that I say nasty things too adds extra weight to the already heavy self-recrimination: why do I talk and behave like an uncivilized brute? Perhaps I am a nasty creature as some people allege, even though I know in my heart of hearts that I am not. My situation could be put in simple terms: I have a problem that I cannot live with, but I do not know how to solve it, and nobody else seems to, either. At best, all I can do is look at others and envy them for being able to exercise the kind of control I cannot; for being the kind of creatures they are but which, alas, I am not. This makes the situation even worse. Why can't I do what others so easily can?

I have said enough, I trust, to ring familiar bells in you. We all go through these types of events and most of us have had similar feelings at some or another stage. We are familiar too with the endless loop these problems generate and the extra burden they place on us. We become the most difficult creatures to live with, especially with ourselves. Somehow, we are very unhappy either with what we are or with what we have become ("I was such a happy kid when growing up") and we endlessly punish ourselves with self-recrimination. We believe that we could be different; we genuinely wish we could change; we have an intense desire to change and tons of motivation to change. Yet, it is all to no avail. The beast simply refuses to change. Why?

To answer this simple 'why', we need to achieve some clarity first. In fact, there are two kinds of problems entwined in the way I have described the situation: (a) there is the problem of my short temper and what to do when I lose my temper; (b) there is the set of problems and feelings generated by the way I think about myself. If you look at the description closely, or investigate how you think about yourself carefully, you will discover something remarkable. *Most of the problems that make our lives painful are those generated by our way of thinking about ourselves.* My short temper does not make my life painful but, instead, what is responsible for that pain is how I think about it. The biggest problem is created by how I think about my existence. I know I am nice and lovable, but my short temper expresses a nastiness that I inherently do not have. Let me call this familiar way of thinking about ourselves 'introspection'. I now want to suggest that *the real obstacle in transforming myself is this process of introspection and not my psychological make up.*

Even though it is important to trace the origin and crystallization of this habit of introspection, I will skip this step here. Most of us brought up in modern cities have made introspection our own by the time we reach the age of 14-16. If we also have the fortune (or misfortune) of going abroad, by the time we reach our thirties we are deeply mired in this mode. It becomes a natural part of us. We have learnt to continuously introspect.

This process of introspection, which I have learnt from the West and that has also been transmitted through the medium of modern education in India, as well as the socializing process abroad, presupposes something about human psychology that is remarkable. The presupposition is that my short temper expresses a unique dimension of myself, and it tells the world (including me) what kind of a creature I am. Consequently, if I want to change and grow or want to become a different person than who I am now, I must transform this short temper and all such unique qualities that I possess but do not like. That is, introspection presupposes that the unique nature of my existence is contained in and expressed by only those properties (like my short temper) that indicate my unique nature. To change myself, I must understand the nature of these unique qualities first; subsequently, I need to consult experts in 'depth psychology' and/or psychoanalysis to tell me how to change myself.

What, then, do I share with my fellow human beings? Basically, I share a biological substratum − genes, cells, body, brain, and so on. Of course, these do influence our psychology, although we do not know exactly how they do so yet. In so far as I am a member of society, current social psychology tells us, I behave in certain ways which mostly do not synchronize with my individual psychology. I share the prejudices of my community; I act irrationally when in a crowd, violently when a part of a mob, and so on. In short, the social and cultural psychologies tell us about the ways in which society and culture influence or determine or condition our behaviour, feelings, and thoughts, which, of course, are mostly different from the way I am. What I am, or how I am, or who I am, is a confluence of the unique properties I have.

As I have said often, this is only one picture about who we are and what we are. This is a story that one culture – Western culture – has produced about human beings. These are not facts either about us or about the way we are, even though we believe in their truth. To use a metaphor, our biological inheritance forms the foundation of who we are. That is, it is the *sub-structure* of our personality. On top of this foundation and resting upon it is a unique *super-structure*. This structure expresses our individual psychology. In a sense, we are this unique structure. Changing ourselves requires changing this super-structure. Introspection involves delving into this structure; depth psychology and psychoanalysis dig deeper and show us how different layers in this structure are related to each other. The lower or deeper we go into this super-structure, the closer we come to the sub-structure only to discover what we share with other human beings. The higher we go, the more unique we become. Thus, in the last analysis, depth psychology and psychoanalysis relate parts of the super-structure to some layer common across either a small group (say, people who have suffered child abuse) or a bigger group (problems typical of teenagers). This super-structure makes us who we are, and a psychological analysis relates some layers or some elements of this structure to other layers or elements from the same super-structure. This is the image behind the process of introspection we are so familiar with.

Two things stand out in this regard: (a) the higher I go in the super-structure, the more unique I become and the less and less I share with other human beings; (b) my uncontrollable short temper, however, is an expression of 'something else', which I share with other human beings even though it manifests itself at the apex of the super-structure. That is why I am unable to do much about it, whereas a medicine works because it directly influences my brain by interfering with the chemicals produced there. Thus, the apex of the structure expresses both my unique nature and 'something else' that is more biological in nature. In that case, my problem is with the super-structure itself: the way I am uniquely me. In short, my problem is precisely what I take to be my uniqueness!

This argument appears as a *reductio ad absurdum* of the presupposition that underlies introspection which I have expressed in terms of sub- and super-structures. On the one hand, I am driven to create and put great weight on the super-structure I have built because that structure expresses the unique nature of my being. On the other hand, precisely this structure, because it is not sufficiently unique makes me unhappy. On the one hand, I aspire to be unique; on the other, no matter how much I try, I cannot be unique enough to earn that sobriquet. This makes my life a living hell. It makes me unhappy. This makes it impossible for me to live with myself. Thus, it appears as though I have no choice other than to consider committing suicide. However, we cannot do that so easily. I have not heard of (m)any people committing suicide because they are short tempered. Clearly, this reason is not weighty enough to motivate me to undertake such a decisive act.

Hopefully, it is now clear why I said that the problem is not about how I am but about how I think about myself: the problem is not with my short temper but with introspection. This *manner of thinking* creates the problem I face, and you cannot blame my existence for that. In that case, we can split the second question raised at the beginning of this chapter (Is there a 'right' way to think about ourselves?) into two sub-questions: is there another way to think about ourselves? *Can we think about ourselves without introspecting?*

A DURVASA?

The Indian traditions, their theories about human beings, and their cultural practices (that still dominate village life) give an affirmative answer to these two questions: yes. Let me sketch the outline of that answer, as I understand it today, using the imagery I used before, namely, that of a sub-structure and the super-structure erected above it. I will continue to use my short temper as the example.

Suppose that I was born a hundred years ago in Bangalore or born in a village in the interior of Karnataka about 70 years ago. Let us suppose too that I had the same short temper and the same uncontrollable tongue. How would my social circle have looked at it and taught me to go-about with it? After umpteen attempts to help me control my temper, after succeeding only to some extent, my parents would have given up the exercise. However, during this process, and because of their successes and failures, they would have given me a nickname: it would have either referred to the sage Durvasa or to Rudra. In any case, my family and friends would know this: Balu has a short temper. But they would have added, "this is how he is, but he means no harm and does not mean the things he says when he loses his temper." As I got socialized, I would learn that even though 'this is how I am' and that I cannot change completely, I would have learnt how to deal with it. I would have learnt that there are multiple ways of expressing anger in speech and that *some are preferable to others*. My socialization would have created a being that one could call civilized or cultured by channelizing certain speech patterns or specific ways of speaking when angry into acceptable and cultivated ways. As I grew older and acquired nieces and nephews, they too would know: "Uncle is short tempered but is otherwise a sweet, lovable and cultivated man." In short, both my social circle and I would have learnt to accept my short temper as an idiosyncrasy. More importantly, this psychological property would have been formed, groomed, and shaped by others. In the same way that someone has a nervous tic, or someone is afraid of spiders, Balu is known for his short temper. My nickname, Durvasa Muni, would precede me, and I would not pay an overly high price for it, provided I guide my short temper instead of being guided by it. The expression of my short temper would stay strictly within the limits taught by my culture. I would have learnt not only to use cultivated speech when expressing anger, I would also discriminate between recipients of that speech. How I would express my anger to a child would be different from what I would do with a stranger, an elderly person, women, my siblings, my friends, and so on. Instead of endlessly 'beating yourself up' because you can't get rid of your anger, your culture teaches you how to deal with it by significantly expanding your repertoire of ways of expressing your anger while at same time putting limits on it. That is what it means to learn to guide anger instead of being guided by it. In other words, I would have learnt to deal with my short temper in ways that would also enable others to deal with my idiosyncrasy. Then I would learn to live with it without being obsessed by it. My society and my culture would teach me that the super-structure that gets built on the sub-structure consists of many such idiosyncrasies and they are not worth fretting about, if it enables others to deal with my idiosyncrasy without taking offence. Everyone, in this sense, is idiosyncratic, and for me it happens to be my short temper.

Notice what has happened in this process. What Western culture would teach me to see as my uniqueness is seen by our culture as a cluster of idiosyncrasies. When we introspect, we are busy with this uniqueness. When we speak and think of idiosyncrasies, we suggest that they are almost inconsequential because there are known and learnt ways of dealing with them. This is one of the reasons why there is almost no introspective literature in India; Indian autobiographies hardly analyse individual motives, desires, frustrations, or hopes, etc., the way Western autobiographies do.

In such a culture, how do you think about yourself, if not through introspection? If idiosyncrasies are not worth thinking about (we only learn to deal with them through channelization), how or what do we think about when we think about ourselves in Indian culture?

The answer is obvious: you can only think about what you share with your fellow human beings (and perhaps even with other organisms). That is, you think about the foundation or the substructure. Reflecting about yourself is to reflect about human beings. To the extent you are also an exemplar of our species, your knowledge of your 'self' is the knowledge that you have of other human beings. If you are vain, greedy, or loving, your reflections are about the nature of vanity, greed, and love. In short, as you go through life and when you think about your 'self', you are thinking about fellow human beings and the psychology which we all share. The further you push this reflection, the more you understand human beings. The more you understand the latter, the more you understand your 'self'.

In short, what Indian culture transmits is this kind of self-reflection. It does not simply tell you that you ought to indulge in such reflections. But if you want to, there are multiple tried and tested ways of doing so. The process does not pain or harm you; it does not make you unhappy. Because it generates knowledge about fellow human beings, your relationships with them become increasingly thoughtful and considerate.

From the contrast I am drawing, we can distil some general guidelines regarding the difference between introspection on the one hand and reflection about ourselves on the other. When are we introspecting and when are we thinking about ourselves? Clearly, the objects of reflection are different: introspection focuses on the super-structure, self-knowledge focuses on the sub-structure. The manner of thinking is also different. Introspection seeks to relate, in a causal or an explanatory fashion, the layers of the structures to each other, whereas self-knowledge focuses on developing hypotheses to account for the sub-structure and its elements. The experience of this thinking too is different: introspection generates pain and such allied emotions; self-knowledge makes you happier. They also exhibit different kinds of movement: introspection generates a loop, and you go around in circles without getting anywhere, returning to the same point repeatedly; in self-knowledge there is clear progress because the nature of the problem changes with each solution. The experience you have of this movement is also different: introspection plunges you down into a bottomless pit, whereas self-knowledge generates a sense of freedom. Even the way you experience your being is different: the more the introspection, the heavier you feel and the more load you must carry. In self-knowledge by contrast, there is a feeling of lightness because the load gets shed on the way and each additional step becomes the lighter for it. In short, we find two sets of criteria above: a cognitive set and another that is experiential in nature.

There is a reason why I have gone into this matter in such detail. *Reflection on experience* is sensible only in relation to non-introspective thinking. Introspection does not make experience accessible; instead, it takes us away from experience. It creates a self-sustaining loop by sending us to a place where experience is impossible but results only in an endless series of imaginary thoughts. When we think, all we do is blame ourselves: recrimination, beating ourselves up endlessly, feeling guilty, etc.

The first step in learning to think about experience the *Indian way,* as I see it, is to break free from introspection and desist from reflecting on thoughts and feelings, etc., as being unique and individual. Then we can come to an understanding of ourselves and our psychologies by discovering how human we are. To understand why human beings react in specific ways is to understand them; we must see our own reactions and responses as the 'facts' of a hypothesis. This is also an activity: we actively learn how to deal with our idiosyncrasies. Growing up as an Indian is to learn these things and transmit them as well.

In a way, you could say that cultivated and cultured people everywhere interact in a civil fashion with other fellow human beings. While true, this is not what I am talking about. The issue is not about how we behave with others socially but about dealing with our internal life. In one culture, introspection of our unique identity is the route; in another, the 'unique' is incidental and contingent. In the West, one deals with internal mental life as an expression of the unique 'self' that each human being has; in India, there is neither an inner self unique to each one of us nor is there a privileged knower that cognizes the meaning of these unique expressions. Keep in mind that I am not contrasting the 'individual Western self' with the 'familial' or 'collective' self of Asians or Indians. Because to say more about this matter would take us too far away from our subject matter, I will continue further without elaborating on this.

PART II

COLONIALISM AND ITS CONSEQUENCES

CHAPTER 7

COLONIAL EXPERIENCE AND COLONIAL CONSCIOUSNESS

Indian culture has been tremendously influenced by a gigantic event in the political history of humankind, namely, colonialism. Quite obviously, we would expect to find some deep intertwining of political theory and cultural psychology when we talk about India and her people. Cultural psychology asks questions about the relationship between culture and psychology – both individual and collective psychologies. Political theory is concerned with the relationship between people, again both individual and collective, and their polity. Of course, the current state of research in either of the two domains does not allow us to raise, let alone answer, any satisfactory question about the relationship between these two domains in the context of India.

Colonialism has been one of the most significant events in the last three hundred years or so. Its importance to political science can hardly be overstated. Yet, as many have said, it has not been adequately theorized as an event. There is a great deal of material on the histories, the effects, and the political resistances to colonialism. Reading it, however, merely increases the puzzlement about colonialism: though it seems to be at the root of all the ills in the modern world, it is not clear how or why that is the case. Perhaps, this has to do with an implicit consensus shared by many: everyone appears to know what it is and most agree about its immoral nature. Colonialism emerges as a self-clarifying and self-explaining phenomenon. Often, criticisms of a colonizer's specific action replace an ethical criticism of colonialism as such. Ethical objections to the role of the British Crown or the activities of the British East India Company do not allow for an automatic extension. That is, such arguments are not a criticism of the project of colonialism in general unless one can show what is unethical about the project itself. To put it in its sharpest form: what is unethical about a project that, among other things, industrialized, established courts of Law, laid railroad lines, and introduced scientific education and modern medicine in the colonies? If we do not address this issue properly, we cannot develop an understanding of colonialism, and we will not be able to understand what its impact has been.

Even though I will not expand on what I am now going to say, I need to say that the question 'what is wrong with colonialism' and some of the answers (building railways, introducing scientific education, the institutions of law, etc.) are far too generic. The answers require further interrogation: when the British introduced the institutions of law, how did they do so? Was the legal system they introduced the legal institution that jurisprudential texts talk about, or did they corrupt that system as it suited their goals, needs and desires? Did we inherit the pristine simplicity of Law or a rotten core with corrupt arms of the law? Answering these questions with any seriousness requires writing a history of colonialism of a kind that does not exist. Hopefully, our historians will begin writing this history instead of the kind they have produced over the last century.

COLONIAL EXPERIENCE

I said earlier that colonialism induces processes which play a role in preventing access to experience. This is *colonial consciousness*. It is time for us to go deeper into this phenomenon.

Colonial consciousness is both a process and an event. It is an event because the colonial consciousness that I am talking about comprises of a multiplicity of actions of indefinitely many people over a long period of time. It is also a process because colonial consciousness reproduces itself; it is transmitted through generations and is itself learnt. Consequently, we need to understand the mechanisms of this process and the structure of that event.

At a minimum, this process must be cognitive in nature. It must be cognitive because it consists of a framework and theories in that framework that deny access to our experience and make us reproduce some sets of ideas as though they describe our experience. It must be cognitive also because, by reproducing descriptions and by embellishing them with details, we act as though we *understand* such descriptions. In other words, the growth and spread of colonial consciousness require a cognitive explanation, i.e., *why do we think we understand colonial descriptions of India and ourselves?*

When we talk about colonial consciousness, we must keep the broader issue in mind. That issue is: what do we 'experience' when colonial descriptions are used by us to understand India? I have called it the 'colonial experience'. Thus, the problem we need to decipher is: what is this colonial experience and how can we understand it?

To begin with, the word 'colonial experience' picks out the experience of the colonial masters and their subjects. When the colonial masters described their experience, they were convinced that they were describing the world and their colonized subjects the way these were. They described their experience in terms of the features and properties of the world. How could the denotation of some features of the world be the same as the description of an experience of the world? Under some assumptions about human psychology, we need to add the premise that unless we are hallucinating, our experience of the world is veridical. That is, unless we are hallucinating, our senses tell us what there is in the world is true. This is a premise that all human beings normally accept. Therefore, in and of itself, there is no surprise that the colonial masters described *their experience* of the nature of their colonial subjects. They experienced Indians as lazy, corrupt, dishonest, backward, immoral, etc. This experience was formulated in terms of the actual features of the world, i.e., as the actual psychological properties of the native Indian population. In this sense, their descriptions were not seen by them as their *subjective* impressions but as wholly objective descriptions of Indian people and their culture. In fact, we can show the wrongness of colonial descriptions only by treating them as objective (and not subjective) descriptions of the world. My research programme, unlike those of others, does not deny objectivity to these descriptions either by suggesting that such descriptions do not describe features of the world or that they express 'racism', 'white superiority', 'Eurocentrism' or any such things. Instead, I guarantee objectivity to these descriptions by anchoring them in the culture of the colonial masters: *the existing descriptions of Indian society and culture are Western cultural descriptions of the experience of an alien culture.* This guarantee is required because it was very much a part of the colonial experience that their descriptions were objective. It is not only the past that demands a guarantee; some of our contemporaries (the intelligentsia) also reproduce colonial claims: Indians are lazy, immoral and corrupt; our social structure is determined and defined by 'an inhuman caste system'; our past is the awful story of oppression of the 'depressed classes' (as the British called them; today, we use a different word) by 'the upper castes'; our present is the result of corrupt, self-serving and inefficient politicians, bureaucrats, police and judges; our future (consisting of development, progress, modernity and secularism) is mortgaged to the immoral and moribund religion called 'Hinduism'; and so on. If the British identified Indian nationalism (even though nationalism is a poison we inherited from the West) with 'terrorism', our modern-day pundits call it 'Hindu fundamentalism', while some from the Left see 'Fascism' in it. We must take such characterizations seriously even when we disagree with them. We can study them seriously only by guaranteeing objectivity to these claims and not by dismissing them as subjective nonsense. What does 'objectivity' mean here? It merely means that if you were to belong to the group of colonial masters, you too would have produced or agreed with their descriptions of the colonial subjects.

Earlier on, I used to think that colonialism sets up a framework that presupposes and thus proves the superiority of Western culture. This formulation is limited because it refers only to 'modern colonialism' (or Western colonialism). So, I need to separate two threads in that thought: British colonialism introduced the framework about the superiority of Western culture that was both presupposed and proved; the imposition, sustenance, and reproduction of such a framework relies on violence. The first is specific to the British in India. The second characterizes colonialism in general.

The colonized accept the colonizer's claims as descriptions of their experience of the world. (There is also another way of saying the same: the colonized subjects accept that the colonizer's descriptions of the world are the 'truth' about the world instead of merely describing their experience of the world.) This gives rise to a crucial question now: if Indian culture differs from Western culture, there must be a mismatch between the way the West describes its experience of Indian culture and the way Indians experience themselves and their culture. So, we can ask: what made Indians think that the British experience of India describes India the way it is? This issue becomes even more acute because of another claim that I have been developing: one of the characteristic aspects of Indian culture has been its continuous emphasis on reflecting on experience. Thus, Indian intellectuals must have been able to see that what the British were saying about them did not match their own experience. Yet, instead of disagreeing, they acquiesced. What made the Indian intellectuals blind to the nature of their own experience? If we assume that events that occurred in the world are responsible for this, what happened in the past that made the intellectuals of India lose their grip on an essential element of their culture? How could Indian culture have failed in accessing its own experience, when its internal focus was precisely on reflecting on experience?

As of now, I have answers to this broad issue in the form of some sub-hypotheses.

One such sub-hypothesis is about the Islamic rule in India. It was not a mere foreign rule but a colonization of India because Islam did not remain foreign to the society it ruled. Instead, it interacted with the society and culture in multiple ways, impacting the culture and being impacted in turn. Islamic colonization did what every colonialism does – deny access to experience. Islamic colonialism also made our own experience partially inaccessible to us and this is where we were when the British colonized us. In fact, the British built on Islamic colonialism: one continued the work of the other, albeit in a different way.

Islamic colonization enabled the penetration of Islamic themes into the ideational world of Indians using Indian terms and words. This was possible because Indian culture was already losing its vibrancy when Islamic colonization occurred. This situation had to do with India's own past, which requires closer study and scrutiny. It was this colonized and weak India that British colonialism encountered when the British East India Company settled on the shores of Bengal.

It is my hypothesis that Islamic colonialism arrested the transmission of many of the theories that had crystallized in Indian culture: our theories about people, society, and nature. By arresting their transmission, by breaking the unity that was established between these theories and our daily experience, Islamic colonialism inflicted violence on the Indian people. In the absence of access to these theories in the way Indian culture was used to, certain aspects of experience lost their intelligibility and could no longer be reflected upon. Islamic colonialism damaged our abilities to reflect on experience and thus made these facets inaccessible to us.

How did they damage these abilities? The answer becomes obvious if we look at the way theories originate: they emerge *explicitly* in intellectual circles and percolate in a thousand ways into the daily lives of people. So, Islamic colonialism must have impacted the intellectual circles; it would have impeded and arrested the growth and development of these theories in intellectual circles.

This colonialism did not merely rule over us and collect revenues. Nor did it merely indulge in forced conversions and the destruction of temples. The rule was not just limited to making Islam a part of Indian culture nor was it finished with the emergence of the Bhakti traditions inspired by Sufi mysticism. This colonialism arrested and impeded the transmission of theories that were required to make sense of our experience. Islamic colonialism cut the link between reflections on experience on the one hand and having such experiences on the other by destroying the fecundity of intellectual life in India. How did it accomplish this? Perhaps, one way of figuring that out is to undertake a different kind of study about what has happened and what is happening in Kashmir, Bangladesh, and Pakistan. There is a peculiar intellectual poverty in these regions if one looks at what the intellectuals have produced there. Today, Sharadamba, 'the Kashmirapuravasini', has become an alien in Kashmir. How did this happen in a matter of 70 years? This too requires further research.

Here is one of the effects of Islamic colonization. By destroying (and thus arresting) the learning and teaching processes of reflecting on experience, Islamic colonialism created a vacuum. In destroying a class of intellectuals, Islamic colonization damaged Indian culture although it did not destroy it. What was destroyed in the process of damaging the culture was both the production of and the capacity to produce our equivalents of Western theories. Such damage is comparable to the impact of the destroying of institutions of learning in the West: it cripples the culture for a time but sooner or later re-emergence is possible. However, India did not find this reprieve because the British colonized us before any recuperation was possible. Islamic colonialism created a class of pundits, who were mostly divorced from the activity of producing knowledge, which, in India, was strictly tied to reflections on experience. Not that pundits did not exist before; they did. However, Islamic colonization transformed them into the only guardians of the Indian traditions. By the time the British colonized India, by and large, these intellectuals had 'forgotten' how to reflect on their experiences. British colonialism marginalized these pundits further by creating a new class of intellectuals who were even more divorced from the activity of producing knowledge that was characteristic of our culture. This is the first sub-hypothesis. Let me now draw out some of its details by using what we have already covered and what I have written elsewhere.

Ideas from Islamic theology began to permeate social and cultural life in India as commonplaces – as usual and ordinary things. This could happen only if Islamic theological themes could be woven into Indian notions and propagated as reflections on Indian experience. Because theological ideas impact cultural lives, the Indian responses were coloured by this theological content. Many traditions emerged at this crossover or cusp where a secularizing religion and a tradition met: the dargahs and the Sufi traditions are examples. The Indian traditions themselves did not remain unchanged. New traditions emerged as responses. Notions of 'God', 'divinity', 'godhead', etc., became central to such responses. So too was a hostility towards the 'other', viz., the traditions and practices of the culture that existed at that time. The 'Bhakti movement' embodied both the tendencies: it appeared hostile to Indian culture of that moment, but expressed a deep fascination with 'God', His 'known' properties, our pathetic human nature, human subservience to His will and so on. This too requires further research before we can understand it fully.

Much later, under the British, we also witness a similar response to the Protestant attack on Indian culture. Many movements such as the Arya Samaj or Prarthana Samaj modelled themselves on the Protestant Reformation (as Indians understood 'reformation', of course) to 'reform' Hinduism. The nature and tenor of the Protestant theologies which they encountered defined their themes and determined their responses. In Indian hands, the 'unknowability' of the Christian God became identical with the 'subtle', 'deep' and 'profound' nature of the Atman or the Nirguna Brahman that the Upanishadic seers spoke about; the Christian 'soul' became the 'Self'; and Krishna was both the 'Judge and the Redeemer' of humankind in the same way as God and Christ represent these two figures in Christianity (as President Radhakrishnan puts it in his commentary on the Gita).

Because what I am now writing is merely a rough outline, some warning is necessary before we go further. It is unclear what the relationship is between the various kinds of Bhakti that we hear about and practice in many parts of India to this 'Bhakti movement', which, according to Western savants and their Indian imitators, is a process against Brahmin priesthood (a trope from Western culture) and the inherent injustices in Indian culture. According to these narratives, the leitmotif of this Bhakti 'movement' is its rejection of the practices and culture that existed in India when Islamic colonization occurred. It is equally unclear if people in different parts of India were identifying the same phenomenon when they spoke of their 'bhaktis'. It is not known to us what relationship exists between the Indian traditions (I will speak more about the nature of 'traditions' soon) and the nature of 'Bhakti'. And so on. Therefore, I would urge you to merely see this as a hypothesis for further research and not some established thesis about the Indian past.

CHAPTER 8

COLONIAL CONSCIOUSNESS AND SECULARIZED CHRISTIANITY

Let us recollect what I have said about experience or *Anubhava.* To transform what we undergo in the world into experience, we need to go through a state-change. I said that: "To become a human being, one must go through an 'apt' process of transition. Such a transition involves learning." I suggested too that things could interfere at that stage and inhibit the processes of state-change and learning. That is exactly what Islamic colonialism did: *it interfered by inhibiting.* Let us see what happens to the process of experience as a result. If an apt transition is not possible and if learning to transform what we undergo in the world into experience is hindered, what happens is that we *lose access to our experience.* A *non-apt* state-change comes into existence and instead of an apt transformation, *a deformed transformation ensues.* Our experiences become inaccessible and are deformed. This deformation denies our experience to ourselves. As I have said, this is colonial consciousness: it denies and distorts our experiences and makes them inaccessible. The question is: *how did this take place?*

To answer this question properly, a deeper and broader *empirical investigation* into our collective past is required than what I have been able to undertake so far. Therefore, I confess that I cannot answer this question. But I have done enough work to suggest a tentative *theoretical hypothesis* that can direct the required research and can be refuted by the results of such investigations.

As I have shown in my other writings, religion expands in two ways. Even though I will mostly focus on Christianity in this chapter, many things that I say about Christianity apply to other religions, including Islam. Therefore, every now and then, I will illustrate a general point about religion by taking Christianity as the example. The first, well-known way in which religion expands is through the direct conversion of people into its fold. 'Conversion' merely picks out the process of inducting new members into a religious community, whether as children born to Christian/Muslim parents (a vertical process) or as adults who move away from one religion to another (a horizontal expansion). Thus, apart from people born into the community of believers, other people from different cultures, religions, or traditions are explicitly converted and the community of believers grows. This is the 'surface-level' or explicit way in which religion expands. In India, both in the colonial and in modern times, this has been a theme of intense controversy but, according to me, it is not of great consequence when compared to the second, more insidious, expansion of religion.

SECULARIZATION

The second way in which religion expands is the process that I call 'secularization'. However, the process of secularization that I speak about is different from what is commonly understood by this term. Let me take the example of Christianity and say what 'secularization' here consists of. I say that Christianity *secularizes itself* in the form of a 'dechristianized Christianity'. Typically, Christian doctrines spread wide and deep beyond the confines of the community of Christian believers into the society at large, dressed up in secular, that is, not in recognizably Christian clothes. We need a small bit of Western history here to understand this point better.

Usually, the Enlightenment period, identified as the Age of Reason, is alleged to be the apotheosis (or the 'zenith') of the process of secularization of Western culture. What people mean by 'secularization' here is the following: the Enlightenment thinkers successfully fought against the dominant grip of Christianity on social, political, and economic life. From then on, the standard textbook story tells us, humankind began to look to reason instead of, say, the Church in matters social, civic, political, etc. This story continues further: the spirit of scientific thinking, which dominated that age, continues to gain ascendancy. As heirs to that period, which put a definitive end to all forms of 'irrational' subservience, we are proud citizens of the modern-day world. We are against all forms of despotism and we are believers in democracy; we believe in the role of reason in social life; we recognize the value of human rights; and we understand that religion is not a matter for state intervention, but a 'private' and personal affair of the individual in question. This is the standard textbook story on what 'secularization' is.

The problem with this story is this: the formidable reputation of the Enlightenment thinkers is built on their opposition to all 'organized religion' or even religion *tout court*. However, these ideas are just a *repackaging* of the ideas of Protestant Christianity, even though they are sold as though they are neutral and rational. Take, for example, the claim that religion is not a matter for state intervention but the private affair of an individual. Indian secularists jump up and down defending this idea. But who believed that religion was *not* a private matter but a community affair? The Catholic Church, of course. Even to this day, the Church believes that you should believe only what the Church says; and because it mediates between Man and God, what you believe as a Christian is decided by the Catholic Church. The Protestants fought with the Catholics against this idea, *on theological grounds*. They argued that 'being a Christian believer' (or what the Christian believes in) is a matter between their Maker (i.e., God) and the Individual. It was God (i.e., the Christian God), who judged man; and men could not judge each other in matters of the Christian faith. Therefore, they argued, the Church could not mediate between Man and God (according to their interpretation of the Bible). The Catholic Church argued that ordinary men, using their reasoning and interpretative abilities, could not interpret the Word of God (i.e., the Bible). To believe that they could was to be seduced by the Devil. The only guarantee against seduction by the Devil, and the eternal damnation that would surely result, was the Catholic Church with its interpretation of the Bible. There is a famous doctrine of the Catholic Church, which says, '*extra Ecclesiam nulla salus*': there is no salvation – i.e., no redemption – outside the Church. To cut a long story short, the Protestants won this theological battle. The Enlightenment thinkers simply repeated this Protestant story, and this has become our 'secularism'. Notice however, that even though Protestant theology removed the distinction that made the spiritual into the exclusive domain of priests, it still retained the idea that there is a two-fold division of the world into a spiritual realm and a temporal realm. Ever since the earliest history of Christianity, it was believed that the world is split into two different realms: the spiritual and the temporal. It is this idea that, during the Enlightenment period, morphed into the idea of separate political domains such as the public and the private sphere.

I am not merely making the point that some ideas have their origin in religious contexts. My point is more than that. I claim that we cannot accept these theories without, at the same time, accepting Christian theology as true. What the Western thinkers have done over the centuries is *to dress up Christian theological ideas in a secular mantle*. The Enlightenment period was the high point of this process. It's not just that they took this or that isolated idea, but wholesale theological theories themselves.

I am not suggesting that this is a conspiracy. I am merely explicating what I mean when I say that Christianity also spreads through the process of secularization. What has been secularized are sets of ideas about Man and Society that I call 'Biblical themes'. They are Biblical themes because to accept them is to accept the truth of the Bible. Most of our so-called social sciences assume the truth of these Biblical themes.

For example, the discipline of religious studies mostly presupposes the truths from Christian theology, even where the writers are not Christians or believers. Thus, when scholars study so-called religions from other cultures, their results are not that different from a theological treatment of Christianity. Our secular ethics are mere secularizations of Christian ethics. That is why, according to these modern secular ethics, Indians are either deeply immoral or resemble moral cretins. According to Christianity, only their 'true' religion can provide a foundation for ethical behaviour; the Heathens and Pagans, because they worship the Devil, are either immoral or intellectually weak. That is, the heathen religion is the foundation of an immoral society and immoral behaviour. Based on this supposition, they found that Hinduism was immoral and, as such, it is the foundation of the Indian caste system, which is also terribly immoral according to them. The social and political sciences repeat this story unfailingly: *Hinduism is the religious foundation of the Indian caste system, which is immoral.* Even in the field of psychology, the notion of 'person' or 'self' and thus its development, according to development psychology's claims, is a non-trivial secularization of the Christian notion of 'soul'. Thus, I can go on.

To appreciate the *plausibility* of what I say, ask yourselves the following: why are the so-called social sciences different from the natural sciences? Why have the social sciences not developed the way the natural sciences have? There must have been many geniuses in the social sciences; some domains are extremely sophisticated, mathematically and logically; today, we have super-fast computers that can simulate increasingly complex phenomena (especially if quantum computers can be utilized in this process). Furthermore, it is not as though social sciences have been starved of funding or personnel. Despite this, the social sciences show no signs of progress. Why? When you have a problem in your relationships, you do not open a textbook on psychology; you look for counsel with a wise friend or an understanding relative. Here is my answer: you cannot build sciences based on theological assumptions. If you do, what you will end up with is *not* a scientific theory, but an embroidering of theology. This is what has happened. Most of our social sciences are not sciences in any sense of the term. They are merely bad but secularized Christian theologies.

QUESTIONS ABOUT SECULARIZATION

This raises some questions: How can these scholars be driven to embrace Christian theology when they either openly reject it or know nothing of it? Why do we, Indian intellectuals, not see this secularization of Christian themes straight away? Why is the process of secularization invisible to Western intellectuals as well?

In a way, the answer can be provided in a single sentence: the research questions and the research framework of many a social science were set up explicitly by Christian theologians using the resources of Christian theology. I am using 'theology' as a general term here. Both the questions and answers have retained their intelligibility, even though the explicit theology has faded into the background. A theological question does not cease to be theological just because the one who answers it does not know much about theology. The very fact that such questions make sense, and do not appear nonsensical, is proof of the fact that the questioner remains within the ambit of a religious framework. If you do not know physics, the question 'when do some stellar objects become quasars?' will not make much sense. To answer it, you need to draw upon the resources of theories in physics.

Fundamental to Christianity is the belief that there 'ought' to be scriptural sanction for actions in the world. That is, this religion makes one seek scriptural foundations for one's actions – whether for sacred ones like worship or secular ones like our attitude towards strangers. The scripture is but one revelation of God's will; Nature also reveals God's Will but in another way. One needs to study both the Good Book and Nature to find out what God's Will is, so that one may be a part of God's purpose for humankind on earth. The Church, as a social organism, confronted many social and political problems during its history. Whether it was a revolt of the peasants, or a fight with the monarchs about the nature of political authority, these phenomena were conceptualized as problems within theology. That is, both how the Church formulated the problems and how it responded to them were inspired by the scriptures and the writings of the church fathers. The problem of state and society, the limits of political power, etc. were actual issues confronted by the Church. These questions and answers along with their underlying framework have been taken over by the so-called social sciences. Thus, when they move further along this track, all they do is further embroider Christian theology. No matter what they think they are doing, they are not doing science. Even when the things they speak of sound totally nonsensical when explicit theology is left out, they continue to talk as though it makes sense.

What I am saying is that Western intellectuals are blind to secularized theology for the simple reason that it is all they know. This is their tool, and they have no other. Only when we develop alternate manners of theorizing about Man and Society will they too be able to see the theological nature of their thinking. Until such a stage, all they can do is to ridicule the suggestion that they are merely embroidering theology.

If what I have said is true, we can see more clearly why the notions of conversion and secularism are jarring to Indian sensibilities. Somehow or the other, Nehruvian secularism always connotes a denigration of Indian traditions; if you look at the debates in, for example, EPW, Seminar, and journals like that, one thing is clear: none of the participants understands secularism. Therefore, they have created a hybrid called 'Indian secularism' and say that it is different from Western secularism. Further, they counter secularism to communalism, whereas 'the secular' in European languages, has only one contrast: 'the sacred'. I do not want to make much out of this; but I thought that it would be worthwhile to draw your attention to this interesting fact.

To summarize what I have said so far: Christianity spreads in two ways: through conversion and through secularization. The modern-day social sciences embody the assumptions of Christian theology, albeit in a secularized form. That is why when we draw upon the resources of the existing social sciences, we draw upon Christian theology. In this Christian theology, we Indians are mostly worshippers of the Devil and our gods are demons. As such, amongst other things, Indian pagans are perverts – sexually, morally and intellectually. The worst of the lot are the priests of the Devil and these are the Brahmins or the 'upper caste' as it is called in India today. The devil-worshipping Hindus are perverts or why else would they follow the Devil or his minions? Even if the social sciences *oppose* a straightforward Christian understanding openly, their *conclusions* are no different from the simplistic story I just sketched. This is an insidious process: *the secularization of Christian ideas*.

MECHANISM OF SECULARIZATION

As we have seen above, *religion secularizes itself* and expands. The secularization of religion is insidious also because it looks as though the secular is in opposition to religion and, therefore, the secularization of a society reduces the impact and control of religion over social and cultural life. My research tells a different story: the secular is also one of the ways of the expansion of religion. It is not the case that a society becomes free of religion as it becomes more secular; *religion expands by secularizing itself*; therefore, society remains just as religious even as it rids itself of the vocabulary of religion. Even though the expansion of religion occurs through secularization, the process of secularization is hostile to religion because of the specificity of religion. Religion is always a specific religion, whereas the tendency of secularized religion is to *universalize* itself, and thereby transcend specificity. This universalizing drive of secularization is constrained by the fact that it secularizes a specific religion and, thus, some specific sets of beliefs and doctrines.

There are two aspects to the secularization of religion. On the one hand, it creates or generates a secularized religious world; on the other, in the world of ideas or the ideational world, it transforms theological or religious ideas into secular forms so that they are not immediately seen as religious ideas.

The three Semitic religions we know, viz., Judaism, Christianity and Islam, are secularized in different forms, even though all three create a secularized religious world and expand in a secular form. Every believer is a 'convert' either when born into a community or when inducted into it as an adult. Religion secularizes itself through violence: violently destroying the 'other' world it confronts within whose womb it is born. This violent destruction of the earlier society is not an accidental or a contingent property of the process of secularization; because this is how religion secularizes itself, that violent destruction of the 'other' continues even when it moves beyond its native borders. Colonialism is also an expression of this violence. Other societies and cultures are attacked with the aim and goal of decimating and obliterating them. Whether the other culture is destroyed or merely survives in a damaged state has to do with the nature and strength of the other culture. The drive and force of secularization tolerate neither the 'other' nor the different. After all, it does not even tolerate the 'other' of its own self which it is secularizing. As noted above, the secularizations of religions are hostile to specific religions because the specificities and the unicity (every religion is specific and unique) of religions limit the universalizing drive of their secularization.

Indian responses to Islamic and British colonization also exhibit how Semitic religions were secularizing themselves. This too must be looked at deeply and closely.

CHAPTER 9

COLONIALISM AND LANGUAGE

The framework that the British introduced did two things. *First*, it secularized the Christian story: it recast Indian traditions in terms of religions; it described Hinduism as a variant of Catholic Christianity and Buddhism as a variant of Protestantism. The 'tyranny of priesthood' was prevalent in India just as it was in all heathen religions, including Catholicism. 'Temple entry' became an important slogan because the British thought that the power of the Brahmanical 'priests' was in their temples and the concomitant priestly powers. Breaking the powers of the 'priestcraft' would be accomplished by insisting upon 'universal entry' into the 'Hindu' temples. And so on. Much of what they said and did can be shown to derive from this process of secularization. *Second*, this story attached itself to the cultural and social reference points present in the daily lives of Indians. By doing so it transformed itself as the core experience of Indian culture.

When the British colonized us and denied us access to our experience, we were already partially denied of it through the Islamic colonialism. British colonialism could build further on the success of Islamic colonization. The British introduced a framework that could thrive in the partial vacuum that the Muslims had already created. Both forms of colonialism denied access to our experience, although each did it in a different way. The British identified reference points

98

(the massive Shastric illiteracy of Brahmins, for instance) and began to generate *ad hoc* explanations of, and reflection about, these reference points. Indians took to these explanations the way ducks take to water because they saw in this framework and its explanations what they were already familiar with: reflections and theorizing about experience. By identifying these reference points within Indian culture, the British created a class of intellectuals who accepted the claims of the British about the caste system, about Hinduism, and Buddhism, and so on.

It is one thing to believe that the description of the colonizer's experience of the world is also the experience of the colonized, but it is quite another to 'discover' for yourself that it is the same. When the two are not the same, there are two ways out: the first is to deny oneself access to one's own experience; and because the mismatch keeps intruding, the second is to transform the description of the colonizer until it rhymes with one's own experience. All the institutions that the British introduced coerced the Indians into living up to them. However, Indians responded to this demand by trying to be what the British said they were. That is, the Indians responded to the British requirements by learning to become what the British wanted, and they did this by using the dominant process of learning they were already familiar with – practical knowledge: *mimesis.* They imitated the British and they did this by satisfying the requirements of the institutions that the British had set up. That means, within the colonial context, a cultural way of learning was used to deny one's own experience to oneself. One became a volunteer in the process, even though the British were inflicting violence by denying the Indians their own experience of the world.

In this context, it would be fruitful to revisit one of the doyens of post-colonial thought, Homi Bhabha. He argues that mimicry is also an expression of the 'resistance' of the colonized to the efforts of the colonizer. As I have said elsewhere, this description of mimicry makes the colonized into immoral creatures. Let me recapitulate the argument here. If the colonized is expressing his *resistance* through imitation, it follows logically that this mimicry is not authentic. Imitation is the cloak that hides his true intention, which is to express resistance. He needs to hide it, furthermore, because he is unable to express it openly. This inability, however, is moral in nature: he does not have the moral courage to express his resistance openly but needs the act of imitation as a subterfuge. He is, in short, a moral coward as well. In other words, there is duplicity, deceit and cowardice involved even in the process of imitation. Writing such a resistance into the heart of the colonized is to write immorality into his core and transform him into a fundamentally inauthentic and unethical being.

My arguments provide a different drift: mimesis, or learning through imitation, is the process of learning practical or performative knowledge. It becomes mimicry when such a learning process entails self-infliction of violence. In mimicking, we become volunteers in denying our own experience to ourselves. Mimicry is not an act of resistance but one of self-alienation.

COLONIALISM, LANGUAGE AND MEANING

We have taken over the descriptions of the British and *transformed* them in such a way that they make superficial sense to us (because they pick out the reference points that the British identified). We have created a demonstrable distance between the meanings and references contained in the colonial descriptions and our use of words. With my research programme, this distance can be known: the words we borrow will have no semantic connection with their meanings in the discourse used by the British and we will not be able to provide a reference for many of these words.

Islam did not fundamentally alter the nature of daily life; having tried to do this, it failed to do so in the initial stages of colonization. What does that mean? People continued to learn languages and transmit them to succeeding generations. But with each generation, these words began to mean less and less because the theories they relied upon to make sense were not accessible to these people (unless in the form of texts written in a dead language). So, under the Islamic colonial rule, a way of going about had come into existence in India: fewer and fewer people knew what they were talking about when they spoke of human beings, life, society, and nature. Sensible words did not signify much any longer.

What kind of words am I speaking about here? These are the words we use today too when we talk about human beings: *manas, raga, iccha, chitta, gyana, buddhi, vikara, bhavana, dharma, paapa, punya, adharma,* and so on and so forth. In short, they embrace what are often called 'the Indic' categories. Already, under the Islamic colonial rule, we developed an inability to identify what these words referred to, what their meanings were, and so on. Our daily language is saturated with these words, but our ability to make sense of them was fading fast under Islamic colonialism.

This is how the British encountered us and discovered that the intellectuals of Indian culture were singularly ignorant of their own traditions. I am inclined to view this as a true description, albeit couched in a Western cultural idiom. The British colonial rule introduced forms of Western knowledge that could thrive in the vacuum already here. The British did something more remarkable. They described their experience of us, and we accepted their experience as truths about ourselves. How could we do this? Because by then we had lost access to multiple facets of our experience already! British descriptions of their experience supplanted our reflections about our own experiences, and the British translations became our translations. It is not that we understood the British or their English well so that we could agree or disagree with their descriptions and translations. Because we did not understand the meanings of the words we used in our daily language, we were unable to challenge their descriptions or their translations. Consider this: today, many of us challenge the translations of texts that the Westerners undertake. Why was such a challenge almost singularly unavailable in the heyday of translations? Why did we have to wait till the end of the twentieth century to challenge the translations of Indian texts? I believe this has to do with the fact that a new layer was added to our colonial consciousness by the British. We ended up parroting both our own languages and English. Yet, we entertain the conviction that we understand both very well. How to understand this conviction?

In a way, the answer is obvious. We have merely learnt the use of words. We know how to use both 'mind' and '*manas*' proficiently. We are at a loss only if interrogated about how we identify either of the two. If our understanding of '*deva*' is shallow, how could we object its translation into a superficially understood 'God'? In other words, we have no way of finding out (if we take our proficiency in our own native languages as a criterion) whether we understand English any better or worse than our native languages. Our grasp of both is equally good, even if equally shallow.

However, it remains the case that we use our native languages with ease and fluency. We use words, whether *manovikara* or *chittashuddhi*, in a way that makes one strongly believe that we know the nuanced meanings of these words. In fact, so strong is this belief that we ourselves believe that we know what we are talking about until we are forced to explain these words. Only then do we feel the embarrassment, even though the tendency is to justify this ignorance by referring to learned tracts on the subject.

AN ILLUSTRATION

If the above sounds abstract, let me make it concrete. For instance, the British said that Hinduism needs reform. When they made such statements, they had a specific set of ideas in mind: Catholicism (and heathendom in general) is under the sway of the priests who rule over the gullible. They do so by pretending that the prescriptions and the laws that they, the priests, formulate are the prescriptions and laws of God. Such human additions corrupt the true religion not only because they are immoral but also because any human addition to the revelation of God is a corruption of the true religion. The British saw exactly such priestcraft in Hinduism, and an attempted 'Protestant' reformation in Buddhism. Of course, they merely said that Buddhism was akin to the Protestant reformation in India without conceding that Buddhism allows one to seek salvation or that Buddhism was as acceptable as Protestantism.

Given the absence of religions in India, there is no way we could have understood the claims of the British, let alone the nuances. However, we twisted and distorted them until they made sense to us. We interpret 'reformation' as the process of introducing reforms (the way one reforms laws or the education system). To us, social reform and religious reform are instances of 'reformation' that we initiate. In the quest for a better system, human beings should undertake both. The clarion calls of the Indian 'religious reformers' of yesteryears or of today is to reform 'Hinduism' so that it suits our modern-day sensibilities. Not only that. Even the 'rejection' of Hinduism has followed the same lines as the belief that 'Hinduism' is too corrupt to be reformed (because of the caste system, say) and that one should leave its folds to seek something better elsewhere like Buddhism or Christianity because they do not support the caste system. That means to say, both the religious reformers and the rebels against the caste system share the same conviction: 'Hinduism' needs reform. It is antiquated, backward and a hindrance to everything that we believe in: equality of human beings, the need for progress and change...

In the process of understanding 'reform' this way, we completely fail to understand what the British said or what they could possibly have meant by this concept. To repeat, they believed that when human beings add things to God's revelation, it corrupts religion. The Protestant Reformation in Europe was a rebellion against additions that the Roman Catholic Church had introduced, like the canon laws, the practice of indulgences, and so on. To those who "protested", these human additions to God's word corrupted the Bible. '*Sola Scriptura*', 'Scripture Alone', they said, was the road to salvation and not the practices and rituals that human beings introduced. Human beings corrupted The Bible by introducing human additions to God's word. The Indian reformers, on the other hand, in the name of reformation, want to delete things from the 'original revelation' and add new things, all of which are the results of human deliberations! In short, they look at 'Hinduism' as a creation of human beings that requires modernization. To the Protestants, it would be an abomination to classify them as reformers of the Bible. However, Indian 'reformers' are totally oblivious to the situation. They repeat the British claims, and, in doing so, they act as though they understand these claims. Yet, when they clamour for the opposite of what the British were doing, they show that they have no understanding of the British criticism of Indian 'religions'. This is an example of what I call colonial consciousness.

Such a consciousness is doubly impotent. It cannot access its cultural experience. Where it does read the *shastras* or uses 'technical terms' that have become a part of our language-use (*atman, chitta, kosha, buddhi,* etc.), it has no understanding of their meanings or references. It is equally impotent to access the outlines of Western cultural experience. Such an impotent consciousness constitutes the class of Indian intellectuals today. Is there any wonder that they fail to produce any interesting reflections on either secularism or political or cultural theory? Is there any wonder they are incapable of bringing about regeneration of Indian culture? Most Pundits in India are fossils created by Islam, who reproduce Indian *shastras* as mantras without making any original contribution. The modern Indian intellectuals, fossils created by the British, reproduce Western claims equally mantrically without being able to make any original contribution to the regeneration of Indian culture.

CHAPTER 10

COLONIAL COMMON SENSE

As outlined above, one aspect of colonial consciousness is the following: in making statements about the colonized, the colonizer thinks that he is describing the colonized. The latter, for his part, takes such statements as true descriptions. The issue is not the authority of the explainer (the colonizer) but the truth-value of these statements. How do we know they are true?

Consider the following set of statements:

1. Indians are dishonest, lazy and dirty.

2. Indians are immoral

3. There is religious conflict in India between the Hindus and the Muslims.

4. There is communal strife in India.

5. India is a corrupt country.

6. Bribes are rampant in Indian society.

7. Untouchability ought to be abolished.

8. A discriminatory caste system is a typical characteristic of Indian society.

9. The lower castes are exploited by the high-caste Hindus in India.

10. Indians are superstitious.

This is a random selection from the common sense of the Indian intelligentsia. Are these statements true because they describe the experience of the Indians or because they are parts of an authoritative body of knowledge? Those who think that these statements describe their experience, those who confirm their truth, those who make a living by peddling these in books and articles, those who do 'scientific' studies to prove or explain the truth of these statements— all share colonial consciousness. We do not believe these statements are true because they are a part of some scientific theory but because we believe they describe our experience. Many have made a name for themselves by selling these descriptions as truths about India that have come into existence after Indian independence.

One can ask: "Why do we ascribe truth value to these statements in the first place, if it goes against our own experience?"

Appearances notwithstanding, this is a question of tracing the history of colonial consciousness. To the extent it requires a philosophical answer, it is deceptively simple: these statements appear to explain experience, if one does not think about them or the conditions under which such statements can be true.

You see, the British had what they called a civilizing mission in the world. They wanted to civilize us too. They found us immoral. We were corrupt. They found that we were uncivilized and dominated by superstition. You know all this; perhaps, you will ask why we need to talk about this today. This is where colonial consciousness comes in. Because today, in 21st century India, we reproduce all these ideas as though the British never left us.

A FEW EXAMPLES

In the West, there are three ideas about Law which function as axioms. The first: all well-functioning societies are founded on Law; if they are not, they ought to be. The second is that Law teaches and educates a people. The third is a corollary of the first two: only thus do a people become a nation. As far as I know, no one has shown the empirical truth of these axioms or proved their logical necessity or argued for their normative indisputability. Yet, their truth-value is undisputed, which is why I said that they function as axioms.

When they ruled India, the British followed these axioms: they tried to educate the Indian subjects through Law, interfered in their festivals and social practices, and the state tried to educate a 'barbaric' people by enacting 'civilized' laws. Romulus is supposed to have given Law to the Romans and thereby made a group into a people; Moses gave Law to the Jews and made a people into a nation; Mohammed gave Law and transformed nations into a caliphate. Therefore, in the British imagination of India, Manu acquires the exalted status of a Lawgiver for the Hindus. It is quite unclear what Manu's supposed lawgiving resulted in: (a) Did it strengthen the hold of a religion, its priesthood, and instil an oppression of the downtrodden? (b) Did it perhaps make 'socially unjust' practices into laws promulgated by a 'porous state' that was not a state at all? (c) Did it create brotherhood among a people because they called themselves *Manava* or, as the Indologists sonorously declare, the children of Manu? (d) Did it create a community that followed the laws of Manu diligently and faithfully over centuries till it became a 'nation' or a people? This Manu apparently performs miracles leaving the other 'miracle workers' (as the Romans said of Jesus) in the dust. Be that as it may, the point is that these axioms are not dated; today, they enjoy the same privilege they did during colonial rule.

(a) Some time ago, the Prime Minister of India launched a programme, called *Swachh Bharat*, enjoining the State to teach public hygiene to Indians. This is strange because most Indians are focussed on their hygiene: many bathe three times a day; even more do so twice, and the most at least once. Most

Indians are also keen on sweeping the floors of their houses at least once a day. Yet, for some reason their public spaces do not enjoy the same attention. Instead of trying to figure out how and why a hygienically oriented people think about public spaces so differently from private ones, the state takes upon itself the role of an enlightened teacher in the business of educating what it considers an unhygienic and illiterate populace. It sets into motion a massive, unwieldly bureaucratic apparatus, imagining that it, the state, can teach the alphabets of public hygiene to the people.

I am not disputing the importance of rural sanitation or urban waste management. These issues are very important and have been neglected far too long. Other countries in the world also have facilities and laws to address waste management. But that is not the problem. The problem is that it is only in India that it is an issue of the State intervention *to teach cleanliness* to the populace.

(b) A few years ago, in Delhi, I was invited to meet some sadhus at the Swaminarayan temple. We were informed that my female students should not accompany me and my other male students because these sadhus practise strict brahmacharya. My students were aghast at this 'discrimination' against women, which increased when they discovered that women are not allowed temple entry during certain hours when the sadhus come to perform *puja*. I tried explaining to them that these practices are not directed against women (or anyone else) but that these are the practices of the sadhus as demanded by the vows of strict Brahmacharya. They were as unconvinced as my colleagues in Europe. To them it was clearly a case of gender discrimination. I am sure that it will not be long before someone in India challenges the practices of the devotees of Swaminarayan in the court.

(c) Often, Indian courts find 'good reasons' to interfere with the practices of a people, as in the past: the Jains are said to violate the law when some individuals decide to leave this world in a way that is respected by their community; the people in Karnataka are not allowed to practice ways of serving in temples and performing their ancient practices because they allegedly violate human dignity; the devotees of Sabarimala Ayyappa are said to discriminate when they do not allow girls and women between the ages of 10 and 50 to enter a temple; one must follow the Muslims and Christians in terms of dress codes while visiting temples rather than appearing in our traditional garb; certain games and practices are not allowed because they are said to inflict pain either on animals or by people on themselves.

The above list is endless. From this perspective, practices of different communities, no matter how old and venerated, ought to have their foundation in Law. Otherwise? Why, they are barbaric, of course. The civilized State will correct these mistakes by punishing the ignorant for practicing centuries-old traditions because these allegedly violate the laws made by the illiterate and the massively incompetent.

When the British came to India, they were convinced about the truth of what their religion teaches them: human beings are put on earth to obey the laws of God. All human societies had some set of laws as their foundation. Living together in a society founded upon God's Laws was the only means through which human beings could do what God ordained them to: worship Him. The same religion also taught them that, in the absence of God's revelation, His original dictates would get corrupted by the Devil. The priests of the heathen religions would tamper with divine laws and the mass of people would be sunk in misery and depravation. Driven by this absolute conviction (irrespective of whether or not it is also obsolete), the British tried to locate the laws that governed Indian culture. Once they located such a text (the laws of Manu), they codified it and insisted that the people of India follow the codification. What united both the Anglicists and the early Orientalists was this idea that Indian culture was founded upon laws; they sought to find the 'most ancient text' on these laws because it would be the least corrupt of all. This idea has its origins in the Semitic religions and their empirical history. Once such a text was 'found' and its standard interpretation codified, Indians 'had to follow' it because they could not be allowed to follow the corrupt vagaries of fluid interpretations by the priests of their heathen religion. Of course, such a situation was bound to have problematic consequences for the British: should these people be allowed to follow their heathen laws, or should one impose upon them the results of Western history? During different periods of time, some or the other faction dominated this debate, but the debates never really died. But underlying this debate was a cultural consensus about the relation between laws and society. In this sense, the judicial system that the British introduced was both alien and native: it was alien because of the notion that some law text is the foundation of society; native in so far as the text was eminently a product of Indian culture.

The introduction of such a judicial system forced the Indians to become volunteers in the process of denying their own experience. Laws took on a status and force they never had in their culture, even if it was their 'own' laws. Indians now had to act as though these laws had the character the British attributed to them. In doing so, they became volunteers in the process of which I have been speaking. The same applies to many of their practices: from sati through hook-swinging. They would be tolerated by the British if one could come up with proofs that these practices were sanctioned by the Indian scriptures. This sent the Indians hurrying to dig into their library to come up with such proofs. In this way, they began to provide a scriptural foundation to cultural practices.

But what if the axioms of the West are not God's own truth? What if a society is not *founded* on Law but sees laws merely as a tool to find reasonable solutions to human conflicts? What if Law does not create a nation, but groups become a cultured people precisely because of the colourful variety of their local practices instead – practices which now are alleged to clash with laws? What if Law does not educate people, but merely regulates reasonable interactions amongst them? What if Law does not dictate how people live or die, but allows old customs and traditions to do their work? All of this does not mean to say that we would be willing to countenance any and all practices just because they are traditionally sanctioned. What I am saying is something different: *allow reason or law to criticize human excesses, but do not make either of the two into a foundation for human interaction.*

What does such a statement mean? It does not defend the practice of slave-owning on the grounds of its ancestry. Nor does it suggest that the practices of a people – which is what traditions are – are immutable. After all, traditional practices, say Ganesh Puja, have adapted themselves well to technology. Human traditions can be criticized if found excessive, but this requires leaving normative judgements behind. We do not countenance an evaluation, rejection or change of a way of living because that way of living supposedly *violates some normative principle* when described in a *specific* way.

Travelling this route requires a belief in the validity, acceptability, and value of one's way of living. The way in which Christians and Muslims dress in their places of worship is not a reason for other Indians not to dress the way they normally do in their temples. How the West arranges its own society is not a knockdown argument for its civilizational supremacy, or a proof of the inferiority of other organizations of social life. While such statements are perhaps abstractly acceptable, the Indian intelligentsia obviously does not believe in their truth. If it did, it would not constantly be seeking the intervention of the judiciary to interfere in human practices that carry the stamp of traditions.

Looking from the outside, which is my vantage point, the Indian intelligentsia is desperately imitating the West. However, apart from its thoughtlessness, this move is not as simple as it appears at first sight. When Indians take over ideas from the West, we must remember that they understand those ideas as cultural beings. The culture from within which Indians look at the West and appropriate its thoughts remain undeniably Indian. As a result, what Indians think the State is and why and how they use courts of law have to do with how *they* understand the West from within the framework of their culture and traditions. What guarantee do we have that this understanding is not flawed? How do we know Indians do not distort meaningful ideas in their attempts to follow Western axioms? Perhaps, even more disturbingly, do we even know whether the inheritance bestowed by the British upon India has an intrinsic integrity instead of possessing a deeply corrupt core?

These are big questions to which no simple answers will do. But they do tell us that we need to come to grips with who we are and how we have managed to organize our ways of living as Indians both before and after the two colonizations.

CHAPTER 11

INDIAN CULTURAL PSYCHOLOGY?

It appears obvious that centuries of colonial rule must have had a very great impact on our cultural psychology. How to assess the extent of this impact? Could we, for instance, claim that what I am describing is not merely colonial consciousness but a fragment of our cultural psychology itself? Could we suggest that it is spurious to make a distinction between 'colonial' consciousness and an 'Indian' cultural psychology that is different from this consciousness? Have we, psychologically speaking, already become a variant of the Western psyche?

Though it is possible that we are already Western but merely wear Indian clothes, I think this possibility is unlikely. Colonial rule did not destroy Indian culture but merely damaged its transmission and modified it. If cultures are configurations of learning and our configuration of learning was not destroyed, Indian culture must have adapted other learning processes. This is my assumption. We do not need to find some original or uncorrupted Indian cultural psychology to make this suggestion. It is sufficient to suggest that a cultural psychology in a culture is formed by different processes and that most of them were not destroyed under colonial rule.

Forming the psychology of the members of a culture is the coordinated task of many social and cultural structures. These range from patterns of family interaction to educational institutions to peer group interactions. Many processes contribute towards this end. Even if each of these were modified under colonial rule, this involved a modification and not their destruction. Consequently, there is a distinction between colonial consciousness and Indian cultural psychology. We have learnt to get by with our colonial consciousness; we notice its presence only vaguely and dimly; but this consciousness is not (yet) a part of the cultural psychology of Indians. Perhaps, one of the specificities of Indian cultural psychology is its accommodation to colonial consciousness. While this argument merely lends plausibility to the claim that we are not yet variants of the Western psyche, it does not establish it. However, colonial rule did generate a consciousness that impinges on the cultural psychology of Indians of today. How is it impinging on or interacting with our psychology?

By way of beginning to think about this process, let us look at the phenomenon of colonial consciousness from a different perspective. So far, I have spoken mainly about two things: (a) use of words from a domain of experience – the domain being our experience of ourselves and our fellow human beings – without being able to provide any kind of reference to these words in our experience; (b) the lack of access to explicit theorizing about our experiences with respect to ourselves and our fellow human beings. What is the significance of these facts to our psychology? How do these facts impinge upon and affect our psychology?

Let's take a look at a situation that is gaining prominence in India as more and more Indians suffer from various mental health issues. There are also multiple attempts to raise awareness about these problems. Many celebrities have spoken openly about clinical depression: Deepika Padukone is one example, Virat Kohli is another. Anyone who has suffered from a nervous breakdown will tell you how it is not solved by simply going to a psychiatrist or taking pills. It requires reflection and understanding. Both from the individual in question and his/her surroundings.

Talking to the young people of today, I discovered that their problems are more acute. English appears to make intuitive sense to them, yet words from this language cannot identify units from their experiential world. Unlike my generation, they are even less familiar with words from Indian languages, either because they do not speak these languages or speak them badly. The point is not that they have become 'Westernized' because their experience of themselves and the world is not Western. At some basic level, I have discovered, there is no difference between talking to my parents and talking to these youngsters even if conversation with the latter takes place entirely in English. Their attitude towards our *devas*, for instance, is as genuine as the attitudes of my parents. When they visit temples, they do not do so merely to please their parents. They genuinely partake of the feeling. Yet, there is a great difference between my parents and them: their Indian experiences are inaccessible to their language and reflections. This is because the emotions of these kids are formed through a language use that requires a different experience of self and personhood to make sense. In these young people, colonial consciousness has taken deeper roots. In other words, even though there is no transformation (yet) of their psychologies and the basic structure remains the same, the thick layer (that appears to become thicker with every generation) of colonial consciousness isolates them from their psychology.

Let me illustrate this very briefly with an example. In the Western conception of man (I know of no theories in philosophy or psychology that do not endorse it), human beings develop multiple desires during their lives: the desire for fame, wealth, power, women, recognition, identity, etc. The desires are indefinitely many, and their ends are also innumerably many. Under this conception, to make a well-formed sentence about desire one must specify the object of desire. That is, 'desire' cannot stand alone without a specification of the object of desire ('desire for what?'). In Western theories about human beings, man is a creature with many different desires – always in the plural.

In contrast, the Indian traditions speak about desire in the singular. Desire has no goal, which is why it can take anything as its end: money, fame, sex, identity, power, status. Desire is limitless and it does not have any specific object as its end; it can attach itself to any and every object in the world. This is one of the reasons why desire is seen to be the root of sorrow. In fact, this claim about desire has been further extended to cover all our feelings. One could retrace the origin of all feelings back to desire or see all feelings as variants of desire. It makes intuitive sense to Indians to (a) speak of desire in the singular; (b) see desire functioning as a sort of a 'hanger' for objects. In other words, desire becomes the hanger on which you can hang any kind of coat, shirt, hat, or trousers.

One of the consequences of this difference is reflected in the way in which we work things out in the two cultures. In Western thinking, the frustration of desires becomes a central problem. Invariably, the world (meaning mostly the presence of other human beings in the world) frustrates the desires of individuals, even though the world is the only known place where desires can be satisfied. The world becomes a hostile place where each person has to learn to live with this frustration. In some post-modern thinking, the 'Other' – who is both alien and inhuman – is at the root of this frustration. This Other denies fulfilment of our desires.

In Indian thinking, on the other hand, the indeterminacy and the limitlessness of desire and the futility of the objects in the world to satisfy it are central. The attention turns inwards, into reflections about the nature of desire. The world has little to do with either desire or its fulfilment. In a way, the world is indifferent to our desire. Other human beings or the finite resources of this planet are not relevant to this issue. Even in a possible world where there are infinite resources, human beings will continue to feel unhappy if they surrender to their desire because desire is unsatisfiable.

To help someone in a mental health crisis, it is necessary to appeal to some basic structure of how a person experiences himself and the world. This structure is the structure of Indian cultural psychology and not just the psychology of the individual.

If a crisis does not come about, we can get by with what we have today. In a crisis, however, we realize, that Indian concepts such as *buddhi, chitta, manas, bhaavana,* which we frequently use, have little or no meaning to us. In the sense that we are unable to use them to *think about* what we are going through even though we use them to 'describe' our actions and feelings. Meanwhile, the concepts from Western psychology do not help us either because we do not have a corresponding experience in the world. Moreover, we do not have direct access to our experiences of the world because we have simply mapped a set of words from our native languages that might have been able to help us onto another set of words that require a different experience of the world than the ones we have. Thus, colonialism (a) prevents the transmission of reflections on experience that ancient Indians had developed, but (b) allows the retention of words that require those earlier reflections to make sense, and (c) forces us to map these partially unintelligible words into a language and theory which requires a different experience of the world than the one we have. Because of this (d) it prevents access to the structure of our experience. Colonial consciousness in India emerges out of a combination of these four aspects.

It is not as though we are watching a science fiction movie where artefacts from an ancient and advanced civilization are discovered. In that case, we would not immediately understand how to use them or what to do with such artefacts. But because our culture has been transmitted to us, albeit in a damaged form, we are not completely clueless. We do have required clues to learn to use the tools and concepts that we have inherited. We are also sufficiently advanced to reflect, experiment and figure things out. We owe a great deal to our grandfathers and great-grandmothers, to our mothers and uncles, to our ancestors individually and as a people, because they have transmitted these clues to us. They have done as much as they could, in exceptionally difficult times, without knowing how or even that they were doing. There is continuity. So, these artefacts are not alien but our own inheritance.

PART III

WHO INDIA IS & IS NOT

CHAPTER 12

ET'S HIPKAPI & EUROPE'S HINDUISM

What did the theory of gravitation do? Apart from describing the fall of bodies on earth, it tied the motion of the planets and the ebb and flow of the seas to each other. This theory allowed us to predict the motion of planets, made air travel and the use of satellites to track movements and weather patterns into reality. In other words, it provided us a way to unify different phenomena. Until then, we did not know that these different phenomena were linked to each other and we only had independent, unrelated, ad hoc explanations for each. This is one of the things that a good theory does – it identifies phenomena that belong together.

The issue before us is this: when the West unified phenomena into a religion called 'Hinduism', were they guided by a theory as well? If yes, the questions are these: did the practices and beliefs that this theory tied together into a phenomenon called 'Hinduism' unify things that do not belong together? Or did the Western scholars merely give an inadequate or incomplete description of a phenomenon containing related entities? Is the 'Hinduism' we know today through standard textbook stories made into a unified phenomenon by a 'scientific' theory? Or did the West describe 'Hinduism' as a religion (thus, as a unified phenomenon) despite or precisely because it had no scientific theory? In my writings, I have shown that the 'theory' that guided Western culture was Christian theology and that, unless we want to say that theology is a science, there are no scientific grounds to claim that there is religion in India, whether it is Hinduism or Buddhism or Saivism or anything else. Islam and Christianity do exist as religions in India, but Indian culture never produced a 'native religion'.

The previous sentence does not mean that 'Hinduism' came to India through the infamous 'Aryan invasion'. Nor by suggesting that Hinduism does not exist, do I say that the beliefs and practices that went into constructing this unity do not exist. What I am saying is that these beliefs and practices, even when taken together, do not constitute a religion that can be structurally unified as 'Hinduism'.

Let me provide an imaginary analogy here. Imagine an Extra-Terrestrial (an ET) coming to earth and noticing the following: grass is green, milk turns sour, birds use wings to fly, flowers have fragrance and decomposed bodies smell foul. Convinced that these phenomena are organically related to each other, this extra-terrestrial sees '*hipkapi*' in them. Not only does this ET see hipkapi as a single phenomenon that contains the above but the presence of hipkapi also explains to him why the phenomenon itself must exist and how its elements should be studied in the future. To convince those who doubt the existence of hipkapi, this ET draws their attention to the visible manifestations that evidence the necessary existence of hipkapi: tigers eating a deer, dogs chasing cats and the massive size of elephants. Each of the above is a fact. However, what this ET does not realize is that neither separately nor jointly do they tell us anything about hipkapi as a phenomenon or provide evidence for its existence. He conveniently ignores that the dispute is about the nature of these facts: how do they become evidence for the existence of hipkapi? When more of these extra-terrestrials visit us and continuously reiterate the presence of hipkapi on earth, hipkapi is not only this 'unified' phenomenon (unified by what?) but also becomes its explanation. Thereafter, to ask what hipkapi is, or even how it explains anything, is to express idiocy: after all, everyone sees this hipkapi, a self-explaining phenomenon.

This is what the Europeans did. The *puja* in the temples, the *sandhyavandanam* of the Brahmins, the *Sahasranamams*, etc. became organic parts of an Indian religion; its 'sacred text' enunciated the *Purushasukta*, which is seen by the 'Hindus' as the divine and cosmogenic origin of the caste system, with untouchability as its outward manifestation. Even though there is some doubt about who these 'Hindus' were, and how this religion dominated the whole of India, it was incontrovertible to them that Brahmins were the 'priests' of this religion and that, therefore, it was a religion created by Brahmins. Dharma and adharma were words in Sanskrit for 'good' and 'evil'; Indian deities and divinities had their Greek counterparts. To the missionaries, we were idolaters worshipping the Devil and his minions; to the emasculated liberal of today, we are mere polytheists. In terms of the analogy I have used, the visitor constructs a hipkapi. To him, it becomes an experiential entity. He talks about this experiential entity, as his fellow-Europeans do, in a systematic way. The question remains: the facts are there, yes, but do they provide evidence for the existence of hipkapi? *Does hipkapi exist?* Indeed, the *pujas* performed in temples and at home, the *sandhyavandanam* of the Brahmins, the *Sahasranamams*, the *Purushasukta*, our notions of dharma and adharma, etc. all exist. Do these facts show us that 'Hinduism' also exists? Do they provide evidence for the existence of 'Hinduism' as a religion? Are they organic parts of a phenomenon called 'Hinduism', even if that phenomenon is not a religion?

I am not suggesting that the West provided a false or wrong description of the social and cultural reality in India. But I do suggest that the unity they created by tying these things together is a problem: *this is a unity only for them.* They created a unified phenomenon because of their own theology. There was no way they could understand us otherwise. In discussions about 'Hinduism', this is the problem. Is 'hipkapi' a unified phenomenon or an imaginary entity? *Is 'Hinduism' a unified phenomenon or an imaginary entity?*

The majority opinion on this issue is clear: 'Hinduism' exists, but it has not yet been accurately described. One scholar might want to call it 'religion'; the other might say that it is more accurate to speak of 'Hinduisms' in the plural (but not in the singular); and yet another might want to use some other appellation than 'religion'; and so on. The post-colonials are willing to concede that Hinduism is a 'construct' but suggest that it 'exists' now. I say that *'Hinduism' is not a phenomenon in Indian culture.* Today, a small minority agrees with me.

Am I suggesting then that these phenomena are unrelated to each other? Or am I merely suggesting that they have a different relationship to each other? Irrespective of my answers to these questions, my claim is this: Hinduism, the phenomenon constructed by our colonial masters, is an experiential entity to them but not to us. In this sense, Hinduism is not a part of Indian culture. It has no existence outside the colonial experiences of India.

A CLOSER LOOK

Let us look at the issue a bit more closely: what kind of evidence can prove the existence of Hinduism? This question is far too important to allow for its dissipation into a mere debating point. If we arrive at a consensus here, we can make substantial headway. At the very least, we can then read the material on Hinduism with our questions in mind. Let me begin by citing some evidence presented by people for the existence of Hinduism and formulate my problems (responses) with each of these.

Claim One: Most of the people in India believe in the existence of such an entity. Their belief is the evidence for the existence of Hinduism.

Response: There are any number of instances where people entertain false beliefs. For centuries, many people believed that the sun revolved around the earth and that the earth was at the centre of the Universe. In Europe, people believed that witches existed; that they performed black magic and had sexual intercourse with the Devil. In fact, people even testified in courts of law to having seen demons. Today, we know that these beliefs were/are false and that even though many people believed in their truth, that conviction does not make a false belief true.

Furthermore, the existence of some phenomenon does not depend upon people believing in its existence. Even when we did not know how many planets there were in our solar system, the planets we know today existed. Not knowing about DNA molecules and their role in generating biological varieties do not make either the DNA molecules disappear or change their role. The same applies to blackholes and quarks.

The beliefs of people are (at best) weak evidence for existence claims. At worst, we cannot determine the truth value of a statement only by counting the number of people who believe in it.

Claim Two: The above objection does not apply to social reality. A social or cultural phenomenon requires that we believe in its existence. For instance, if no one believed in untouchability, it would not exist. Here, beliefs determine whether phenomena exist or not. If people did not believe that Delhi was the capital of India, it would not exist as the capital of India.

Response: We need a special kind of evidence if we want to apply this argument to Hinduism. As a first step, we will have to show that all 'Hindus' or all 'Indians' or all the people on earth believe that 'Hinduism' exists. How do we settle this issue? Through a poll? Second, we must show that the existence of Hinduism is something like untouchability and not, say, something like the earth or the moon. That is, we must show that 'Hinduism' is created by human beings. Some people have indeed assumed this to be true, but all of them also assume that Judaism, Christianity and Islam have God as their author and creator, whereas Hinduism has people as its author, viz., it is a 'popular' religion. In that case, it logically follows that if Semitic religions are what religions are, namely a revelation of God, then 'Hinduism' cannot be a religion since it takes God to create a religion.

In fact, the reason why we are considered as idolaters and devil worshippers by the believers of the Semitic religions is because 'Hinduism' is not God's revelation but a human creation instead. It would be wise not to use Semitic theology as evidence for the existence of Hinduism as a religion.

Thus, our problem does not disappear even if we accept that social reality exists if enough people believe in its existence.

Claim Three: Many people from other times and places have registered the use of the word 'Hinduism' among Indians.

Response: Apart from the objection that arose in the context of the first evidence, there is a weightier matter at hand. None could have registered such a use because 'Hinduism' is an English word and is of recent origin. No confusion about the words 'Sindhu' and 'Hindu' will ever give us a *religion* called 'Hinduism'.

Counterargument: The point is not about the use of the English word 'Hinduism'. The presence of its equivalent in other languages has been registered.

Response: If the reference is to other European languages, the problem recurs. If equivalent words are used in non-European languages, one must first *demonstrate the equivalence*.

The usage of a word does not prove the existence of a phenomenon; nor does the absence of words disprove the existence of phenomena. That we use the English word 'unicorn' does not prove its biological existence; that the word 'gravitational force' is of modern origin does not prove that there was no gravitational force exerted on Earth before Homo sapiens sapiens emerged on Earth.

Claim Four: 'Hindu' (*Yin Du* for instance) is used by Indians from an exceedingly early period.

Response: It is not clear whether the word refers to a people, a region or something else. However, using the word 'Hindu' is not enough: one must derive this word from 'Hinduism'. That is, the usage must say that one is a Hindu because one belongs to Hinduism as a religion. Only then will the use become evidence.

Then, the problems (1) and (3) return with a vengeance.

Claim Five: People have been studying 'Hinduism', talking about it, and teaching it. How are these things possible if Hinduism did not exist?

Response: People talked about witches, their alleged intercourse with the Devil and the causal effects of phlogiston. They wrote books about them, people were burnt at the stake because of this issue, legal trials were conducted, and so on. None of this is evidence for the existence of these phenomena. Harry Potter novels, despite their popularity, do not demonstrate the existence of Hogwarts, a magical school.

This is a variant of the first problem.

Claim Six: It unifies Indian culture (or at least some parts of it), and its people. Hinduism creates a nation. The existence of a 'Hindu Nation' is evidence for the existence of Hinduism.

Response: If we want to accept the above statement as true, we need evidence for its truth. Moreover, how do we know that India is unified because of Hinduism? Are Hindus a 'nation' the way the Bible says that the Jews are a nation? What makes a people into a nation is their religion. Our discussion is precisely about this 'religion'. Answers cannot be presupposed as true when they must be proved.

To do so is to commit the fallacy of *petitio principii*: assuming the truth of a proposition that must be proved to be true.

Claim Seven: Most of us can make a list of things we intuitively associate with the phenomenon of Hinduism. We would not have similar intuitions if the phenomenon did not exist.

Response: What happens when intuitions conflict? For example, Europeans claimed that the 'evil of the caste system' and 'dowry murders' are integral parts of Indian culture. Some Indians agree with this judgement intuitively, whereas some other Indians disagree with this intuition vociferously. How do we arbitrate in such cases?

The first problem also recurs.

Claim Eight: Our many acharyas, our grandmothers, and we would agree with a minimal list of what 'Hinduism' is. Thus, the agreement stretches across generations. This consensus is our evidence.

Response: Until and unless one produces such a list and solicits agreements on such a list, the claim is empty. However, that we would agree to such a list is not sufficient. This list must be shown to contain things that make 'Hinduism' into a unified phenomenon that is also a religion. Otherwise, the list would merely show that there are 'some things' we all agree upon. How does this consensus provide evidence for Hinduism?

Problems (7) and (1) recur.

Claim Nine: There are university courses, PhD programs and writers of repute writing on Hinduism.

Response: Similar things can be said of proof for the existence of God, the presence of extra-terrestrial life, parapsychology, and creationism. What do these prove?

Claim Ten: American Hindus passionately believe in Hinduism.

Response: This could be traced to the impact of the Semitic religions on American culture and its impact on Indians living there. In any case, the belief of the NRIs in America cannot make Hinduism exist in India.

Claim Eleven: Hindutva would not be possible without Hinduism.

Response: This presupposes as true what requires proving. The burden of proof is the other way: one must show that Hindutva comes into being because of Hinduism. The alleged 'Hindu-ness' of the word is not an evidence for the existence of a religion, whatever else it might mean. For instance, it could refer to the essential or determining properties of a 'Hindu', which might or might not include belonging to 'Hinduism'.

Claim Twelve: Hindus are persecuted for being Hindus in places like Pakistan and Bangladesh. Doesn't that show that Hindus exist?

Response: That 'Hindus' exist is not a proof that Hinduism exists. The problem of (4) repeats itself. Second: that such people are persecuted does not tell us that 'Hinduism' exists. Third: it shows that Islam (Christianity and Judaism) thinks that 'Hinduism' exists. Should we say that Semitic religions determine which objects exist and which do not?

Claim Thirteen: Indian Law discriminates against Hindus. The Indian constitutional clause about religious freedom, etc. is used against Hindus. We are trying to gain equal protection and rights under such. Now you say that Hinduism does not exist.

Response: Ideally, we should be capable of writing a more intelligent constitution than the one we possess today in India, which was fully modelled after what the British wrote and what a bureaucrat (called Rau) made of it. However, when we use the provisions of a law or statute to fight for our right to exist and not to be discriminated against, this does not prove that Hinduism exists. When we follow the law, we do so even when that law is foolish. But this is not a proof for the existence of Hinduism. A foolish lawgiver's 'will' does not establish objects in the world.

Counter-argument: Why does it matter? Whether 'Hinduism' exists or not, 'Hindus' are persecuted. Whether 'Hinduism' is actually a 'religion' or not, we have to fight for the rights of Hindus, their temples and practices under 'religious freedom' laws across the globe. What does it mean for something to exist other than these things? What is the point actually?

Response: In modern Europe, women were persecuted because they were accused of witchcraft and sleeping with the Devil. Ronald Regan, an ex-president of the US, claimed that the Taliban were freedom fighters and not terrorists and showered them with money and military support. That such events exist and will continue to exist cannot prove or disprove the existence of phenomena. In both cases, the belief about existence of witches and freedom fighters generated actions. That people believe in their existence is not evidence for their existence. The point, simply, is this: is Hinduism a phenomenon in the world? Does it exist? If it is not, we can at least try to figure out who we are if we are not 'followers' of a religion.

These are some of the arguments I have encountered. There is no point, I trust, to go on building such a list.

Now comes the interesting issue. Could we provide a different description of Indian culture? Would such a description tell us what exists in India, and which of the above are related to each other and explain how they are related to each other? Yes, we can. But to do that we must leave the current framework, which we have imbibed through Western scholarship, behind us. Not only do I believe that a different description is possible but also that it is cognitively superior to the received view.

All we need to realize is that there are no 'obvious' answers to questions about the existence of Hinduism and this alone is sufficient to begin asking questions about what exists in India. In the next chapters, I will take the first step in answering the question. Though not a full answer, it attempts to show what is interesting about the 'existence' question and how we could go about conceptualizing Indian culture differently than the West.

CHAPTER 13

WHAT EXISTS IN INDIA?

The peoples colonized by Western culture share a common experience: we fall silent as though our lips are stitched together, and we are as mute as human beings can ever be. Many of you will resonate to the following: your child comes home from a playground or from school almost in tears from the humiliation of losing an argument. When the child narrates its story and says, "I didn't know what to say", the mother or older siblings say, "next time say this" and show them a route to follow. The sense of humiliation and failure lifts, and the child now looks forward to the sequel to the lost argument.

The ensuing chapters contain examples of answers, potential routes, and suggested solutions to some problems. They are versions of 'say-this-the-next-time'. Think about them, connect them to your experiences, make them your own and use them. And where you can, indicate to someone else these potential routes as well.

While reading these chapters, we must keep this context in mind. Many intellectuals in India and in the West have transformed some of the multiple Indian traditions into a single 'religion' called 'Hinduism'. The problem does not lie in trying to unify variety and diversity into a unity. Rather, it lies in trying to fit traditions into the straitjacket of 'religion'. While it might be convenient to call yourself a Hindu, the danger lies in developing doctrines, theologies, catechisms, and commandments of our own to identify a set of people following a religion called Hinduism. These reflections are also applicable to Buddhism, Jainism, Saivism and all such entities. In this chapter, I will not look at the compulsions that force us to manufacture 'Hinduism as a religion'. Instead, I will focus on the nature of our traditions.

ON UNDERSTANDING TRADITIONS

If someone asks, *what is Hinduism?* tell them that there is no such entity in the world outside the universities in the West and in the minds of Indologists. Tell them that when you call yourself a 'Hindu' (for the sake of convenience) that is *because you continue your ancestral traditions.* Tell them too that you are "keeping faith with your fathers, who kept faith with their forefathers, and were blessed in so doing." Tell them also that you need no 'reason' to keep your ancestral traditions alive and that *the only reason to practice a tradition is the fact that what is practiced is a tradition, and that is what it means, as it has always meant, to be a Hindu.*

In the first instance, this is what traditions are and this is how we learn them. They are simply some sets of practices that our parents have passed on to us. The notion of 'practice' is wide: they range from stories through visits to temples to performing rituals. They include the swamis, the *muths* and the Gurus, if and where they exist, but can continue to do fine without these as well. To put it simply, *traditions are inherited practices.*

How are they transmitted? In a variety of ways: through language, through imitation, through instruction, through repeated performances, and so on. There is no one right way to transmit a tradition any more than there is one preferred manner of doing so. The variety of ways is necessary because tradition does not refer to the presence of some specific component but picks out a totality. In fact, some or the other component could either be missing or barely present in a tradition; such absences do not make it any less of a tradition. Attempting to encapsulate traditions as 'beliefs' or 'rituals' or 'festivals' is to distort their nature.

What exactly is transmitted by a tradition? Traditions are structured or well-knit wholes. This gets *transmitted.* Even when we assume that we are transmitting a set of practices from time immemorial, in principle, there is no way of establishing the truth of this belief. If we look at India, we believe that some rituals, some *mantras,* or the ways of reciting the *Vedas* are accurately transmitted from generation to generation. We might even have good reasons to believe this because of the *pathashaalas* and their teachers. However, we can go no further than this. Mostly, our grandparents and our parents transmit practices: there is little external authority to go by. Changes are bound to have occurred; practices would have adapted themselves to ways of living. In this sense, *traditions are extremely dynamic and flexible.* So, we receive our inheritance in the belief that it is our tradition. We modify here and there what we receive and transmit it to our children. Traditions live on precisely because of this adaptability; they are dynamic in their nature and are *never static.* Thus, the claim that being a 'traditionalist' is to be a fossil and to be an 'anti-progressive' (whatever that means) is as false and as silly as the suggestion that 'traditions' should undergo an antithetical process of 'modernization' or that they cease being traditions because of the impact of modernity.

Who belongs to a tradition? Consider the fact that my father never performed any of the daily rituals, hardly visited temples and had an indifferent attitude (for a long time) towards festivals and celebrations which my mother performed. Consider the fact that I continue in his footsteps, and additionally have smoked and have consumed all varieties of meat and alcohol, but unlike my father or my mother, I have made a deep study and done research into the Indian traditions and culture. Do I belong to the tradition of my parents or not? Quite outside of the fact that there is no authority to pronounce on this issue, our traditions allow even such people as my father and me to belong to the Indian traditions. Belonging *to a tradition is a fine-grained affair*; it is not an all-or-nothing situation. When born into one, there is no way of determining who belongs to a tradition and who does not. By the same token, people not born into a tradition can also be inducted into it. The criteria of induction are fine-graded affairs as well.

However, all of this does not suggest that traditions are either fluid or amorphous. They are anything but that. It is extremely important *that traditions be able to distinguish one from the other as a tradition*. The *Lingayat* tradition is not just a *Shaiva* tradition; the *Vishistaadvaitins* are not mere variants of *Advaitins*. Each is not only distinct and different from the other but also strives to retain the distinction. While *Advaitins* say that 'the self is Brahman', they do so by *being different* from *Vishistaadvaitins* who say that 'all is Brahman'. *Being different from other traditions is crucial to being a tradition*. To a large extent, the vibrancy of a tradition is indexed by the extent to which it can retain its difference from other traditions. Today, we are not yet able to make sense of the presence of these two properties: (a) the enormous flexibility in belonging to a tradition and the sharpness with which the boundaries are drawn between traditions; (b) the possibility that any element could be absent from a tradition and yet it can maintain its identity, structure, and distinction. Depending on what we emphasize, traditions appear very elastic and extremely dogmatic at the same time. If we use these terms of description, we describe traditions as variants of religions or philosophies. However, they are not: traditions are neither religions nor are they philosophies; they are what they are – traditions.

Why practice traditions? Though this question appears reasonable at first sight, it is not: it is both loaded in favour of the Semitic religions and ill-formed. To understand why it is both, we need to take a short detour.

Suppose that you come across someone who says, "I have no reason to live." Would the recommendation "go and commit suicide then" be apt in such a case'? Quite apart from humane considerations, there is one reason why the response would fail to be appropriate. It commits a fallacy: from the claim that one does not have a reason to live, *it does not logically follow* that, *therefore*, one has reasons to commit suicide. Even if one does not have a reason to live, one can continue to live; an independent and different reason is required to commit suicide.

In more general terms, a practice does not require a separate reason or justification for its existence. In the same way we do not require a reason to continue to live, we do not need a special reason to continue a practice. The existence of a practice is its own justification; the only reason to practice a tradition is the fact that what is practiced is a tradition. So, those who ask us, "why practice a tradition?" are asking us to commit a fallacy when they presume that one needs a 'special reason' for continuing a practice. This makes the question ill-formed. But there is something else present as well. They are asking us "why ought one continue a practice?"; "why is it obligatory to continue a tradition?" The answer is simple: there is no compulsion or obligation; there is no 'special' reason why one ought to continue a traditional practice. The response of your parents or grandparents when you were twenty or older on why you should go to the temple or why you should perform rituals are relevant here. They merely shrugged their shoulders, even if unhappy with your attitude. Moksha is not denied to you if you do not go to the temple or fail to celebrate Ganesha Chaturthi. This is also the answer to the query, "why ought one to do *puja*?" There is no special or specific reason or moral compulsion that obliges you to continue practicing your inherited tradition.

Thus, to the question, "why do Ganesha *puja?*" the following is an answer: "Because I have learnt to do this *puja* at home." "Why wear *bindis?*" – "we wear them because it is our practice." *Nothing more is required.*

Does that mean that all practices are justified because they are ancestral practices? (For example, meting out inhuman treatment to fellow human beings: is this justified because one's ancestors did something like this?) No, this claim does not follow logically: if there are good reasons why we should abandon or modify a practice, if we are reasonable, we either modify a practice or abandon it altogether. *Reason functions as a brake on excesses of human practice.* No Indian tradition has ever denied this crucial role to reason.

For instance, are sati, child marriage, and such like a part of some of our traditions? Yes, they apparently were. Do they continue to be a part of our traditions? As far as I know, sati is not; but my mother did get married at a young age, my grandmother at an even earlier age, and my aunt was 12 when she got married. However, the marrying age of my sisters changed over time. My eldest sister got married when she was 16, but she was also the last in my family to be married off so early. My parents ensured my other two sisters had multiple university degrees, were employed and therefore financially independent before they got married. As I have said, reason curtails the excesses of human practices and my mother decided to abandon the tradition of marrying her children off early because she said, "times have changed." My sister married her children off when they were in their thirties and I have let my children decide when and with whom, and even whether they want to marry. Modifying or abandoning a traditional practice is an individual choice made, hopefully, on reasonable grounds. However, we do not even need a reason to abandon a traditional practice because one is not obliged to practice it in the first place. A shrug of the shoulders would do as an answer to the question, "why do you not do Ganesha *puja?*"

Following a tradition is unlike following a moral injunction. When one says sati, child marriage, dowry, untouchability, etc. are followed in India because they are a part of the Indian traditions one treats these practices as 'practices that ought to be followed because our ancestors practiced them too'. This is how the colonial and Western mind interprets tradition and 'practice'. To them, following a tradition is akin to following a moral obligation written down somewhere. When speaking of 'following a tradition', Western Indologists are willing to make the concession that we follow oral texts. To them, justifying a practice by referring to an age-old practice is equivalent to justifying a practice ethically. They are not able to think in any other way because they are captivated by the idea that religious texts, whether written or oral, impose moral obligations on us, and we must obey them. This understanding, or rather this misunderstanding of tradition makes these Indologists come up with silly stories and even sillier questions about the nature of the Indian traditions.

What Differentiates Religion from Tradition? A Jew, a Christian and a Muslim worship their Biblical God in certain ways because this God has imposed on them the obligation to do so. In the worship of idols, icons and images, they see only Devil-worship. Their God has told them that if people worship the Devil, they will rot in Hell for all eternity.

If someone believes that these claims are true and does not want to rot in Hell, such a person has good reasons not to do *puja* to *Ganesha*. To a believer and a practitioner of these religions, idol worship is a sin because God has forbidden it and promises that those who practice it will suffer the ultimate punishment: condemnation to Hell. So, we can imagine them telling us that idol worship is one of the greatest sins. But *their* good reason not to do *puja* to Ganesha is not a good reason for *us* to abandon doing the so-called *murthi puja*. It is a part of our tradition to do *puja* to the statue of *Ganesha* and we do it because it is our tradition.

That traditions are inherited practices means two things: they are transmitted and are learnt. Consequently, traditions 'change' (i.e., undergo modifications) even as they are being transmitted and learnt. This makes traditions flexible and adaptive. Human practices conserve: that is, we do not go around inventing new practices every other day. In this sense, traditions are essentially conserving in their nature. This is one reason why we see 'being traditional' as 'being conservative' as well.

Because learning is an individual affair, the individual decides which practices must be modified, which must be retained, and which should be abandoned altogether. Such changes might occur through reflection, in discussions, due to advice from others or because of the sheer impracticability of continuing a practice. In other words, changing the tradition is an intrinsically individual affair. By the same token, what counts as tradition and what does not is also an individual affair. Individuals recognize some practices as traditions and to some extent this varies from individual to individual. This situation is recognized by those who follow traditions: "this is the tradition in our family."

Thus, what counts as a tradition and what does not is independent of providing some criteria beforehand. Any inherited/ modified practice is a tradition, or it is not: that depends on how the individual views it. Do we practice a tradition when we drink water? That depends. While some people drink beer in Europe when they are thirsty, I drink water under similar circumstances. Drinking beer or wine while thirsty increases my thirst, whereas it is common to notice people enjoying beer as an antidote to thirst during warm summer afternoons in Europe. They do this sitting on terraces outside a café, preferably drenched in sunshine. Is this a tradition? To those to whom it is a tradition, it is one; but not to those to whom it is not.

From all the learnt/inherited practices, individuals might call a subset of these as a 'tradition'. Several such individuals might have overlapping sets of practices and many might create more distinct subsets. Most of us cannot enumerate what our traditions are, even if we are willing to call only some of these practices as our tradition. Is wearing a *banian* and a *dhoti* at home also a 'tradition'? One could go either way: to some, it is. To some, it is not. While we are willing to recognize that wearing an *angvastram* on the upper torso was the tradition of our grandparents, we might or might not want to call our fathers wearing a *banian* a tradition.

Human practices do not come with labels attached that identify only some practices as traditions and call others non-traditions. Individuals identify practices that they consider important as 'practicing a tradition' or as 'a traditional practice'. Perhaps, during our lives, we also learn how or why we isolate some practice as important. However, the circumstances in which individuals find themselves vary. Singing in a particular *tala* and *raga* might be considered a tradition by a music teacher; another teacher might not think this way. To those of us who are not musicians, perhaps, this issue is a matter of complete indifference. In short, profound though it might appear, the question, "which practice is a tradition"? is not interesting. Who gets to decide whether a practice belongs to a tradition or not? The individual, to whom it is a tradition. Do they need a Guru or a Swami to decide? That depends not on the practice but on the individual. For instance, some individual might want to consult swamis on issues relating to *puja* in the US; yet others might not, and decide on their own. We might defend both these as traditions as well. Why do any of these issues matter?

Traditions vary from individual to individual while retaining, at the same time, a recognizable pattern and structure when we look at them inter-individually. This has to do with the fact that individuals learn, and that learning is creative; and with the fact that what one learns is a practice which conserves.

The first step in answering a question is to understand it. Most who give 'symbolic interpretations' of our traditions while answering questions about our traditions do not understand the question. In fact, I would go one step further: if you hear people giving profound-sounding interpretations that appeal to symbolism, you can assume that they have no idea what they are talking about. In an extremely simplified form, I will give you the background to help you understand why I make this bold claim. This will hopefully help you comprehend the questions that you get about your traditions.

Consider the Semitic religions. The believers worship their Biblical God in certain ways *because* this God has imposed on them the obligation to do so. Thus, according to them, we exist on earth for one and one reason only: to worship and obey (the Biblical) God. This is the sole purpose of human existence. If people fail to do so, they go to Hell for all eternity. Therefore, they have a 'reason' to worship their God. His Commandment is to worship *only* Him and in *the way* He wants to be worshipped. How do we human beings know *how* He should be worshipped? This is where the Revelation comes in. He has told us how He should be worshipped in "the Scriptures", which are the word of God. To believe in the word of this entity is to hope for salvation; not believing it is to be doomed to Hell for all eternity.

That is, even those who participate in their religion because of their upbringing, the mediation of their parents or their social environment, believe that one needs a *reason to continue practicing* a religion (e.g., "why follow the Biblical commandments?"), or switch between religions or become atheists. Because this is how *their* religions are, they think all human beings think along these lines and they want to know what Hindus believe in. They think that Hinduism is a religion like theirs and that Hindus too have 'Scriptures' the way they have their own. They think that the *puja* of the Hindus expresses beliefs about how God ought to be worshipped. They further believe that the Hindu priests have massively spread disinformation to the masses about God's message as to how He should be worshipped. Who says 'fake news' is a recent phenomenon? According to the Semitic religions, the 'priests of Hinduism', namely, the Brahmins, have been propagating 'fake news' about God and His worship for more than three thousand years. The images of our Devas and Devis that we hang on our walls or sculpt in our temples are 'deep fakes', according to these religions.

We could ask now: what kind of reason does a human being need to be religious and remain one, according to the Semitic religions? Here, there is no better candidate than Truth. One practices a religion because that religion is true. If the temple of Solomon was never built and Moses was merely a fabrication of human imagination, if Jesus of Nazareth did not exist and was never crucified, if Mohammad turns out to have been born in India and never went to the Middle East, then the Semitic religions would simply cease to exist. *The claims of these religions must be true* if they are to remain religions at all. There are two important aspects to this: (a) the followers of these religions need to believe these claims; (b) they believe them because these claims are true. 'Truth' appears as a sensible predicate with respect to religion.

In contrast, how is it with traditions? Until about three decades ago, until, that is, people started transforming 'Hinduism' into a pale variant of these Semitic religions, the answer would have been pretty much the same all across India: "I do not know whether Rama and Ravana existed a couple of thousand years ago; their existence or non-existence does not matter to me for Ramayana to be true." (Of course, the attempt to portray Hinduism as a religion did not begin a few decades ago; it began under Islamic and British colonialisms. But I will neglect that for the time being.) Consider this beautiful dialogue between a Balinese Hindu and a Swiss German precisely about this question. (From Bichsel, Peter, 1982, *Der Leser, Das Erzählen: Frankfurter Poetik-Vorlesungen*. Darmstadt und Neuwied: Hermann Luchterhand Verlag. Pp. 13-14. My translation and italics):

> When I discovered, or when it was explained to me, that Hinduism is a pedagogical religion, namely, that in so far as the best "good deed" of a Hindu consisted of explaining something or the other, I lost my inhibitions and began with questions …

> A young Balinese became my primary teacher. One day I asked him if he believed that the history of Prince Rama – one of the holy books of the Hindus – is true.

> Without hesitation, he answered it with "Yes".

> "So you believe that Prince Rama lived somewhere and somewhen?"

> "I do not know if he lived", he said.

> "Then it is a story?"

> "Yes, it is a story."

> "Then someone wrote this story – I mean: a human being wrote it?"

> "Certainly, some human being wrote it", he said.

> "Then some human being could have also invented it", I answered and felt triumphant, when I thought that I had convinced him.

> But he said: "It is quite possible that somebody invented this story. But true it is, in any case."

"Then it is the case that Prince Rama did not live on this earth?"

"What is it that you want to know?" he asked. *"Do you want to know whether the story is true, or merely whether it occurred?"*

"The Christians believe that their God Jesus Christ was also on earth", I said, "In the New Testament, it has been described by human beings. But the Christians believe that this is the description of reality. Their God was also really on Earth."

My Balinese friend thought it over and said: "I had been already so informed. *I do not understand why it is important that your God was on earth, but it does strike me that the Europeans are not pious.* Is that correct?"

"Yes, it is", I said.

Of course, this attitude towards the Mahabharata and the Ramayana is more intriguing than I can get into here. But let us notice that those from the 'true' religion have great difficulties in understanding such an attitude. They are convinced that Indians believe in the truth of their puranic stories and that these stories replace their histories and geographies. That is why Sir Babington Macaulay, in his famous minute about the need for a British education system in India, spoke in these terms:

It is, I believe, no exaggeration to say that *all the historical information* that has been collected to form all the books written in the Sanskrit language is less valuable than what may be found in the most paltry abridgements used at preparatory schools in England. In every branch of physical or moral philosophy the relative position of these two nations is nearly the same ...

The question before us is merely whether … we shall teach languages [Sanskrit and Arabic] in which, by universal confession, there are no books on any subject which deserve to be compared to our own; whether, when we can teach European science, we shall teach systems which, by universal confession, whenever they differ from those of Europe, differ for the worse; and whether, when we can patronize true philosophy and sound history, we shall countenance, at the public expense, *medical doctrines which would disgrace an English farrier – astronomy, which would move laughter in girls at an English public school – history, abounding with kings thirty feet high, and reigns thirty thousand years long – and geography, made up of seas of treacle and butter* (cited in Keay, John, 1981, *India Discovered.* London: Collins, 1988: p. 77, my emphasis).

Did Indians ever believe that seas of butter existed in some part of India (say in the Chennai of today) some two thousand years ago on which the Indians set sail to discover other parts of the world? Did they ever believe that a few thousand years ago, kings thirty feet tall moved around (say in the Delhi of today)? How Indians *talk about their past* cannot be collapsed into *beliefs about the truth* of their past without making them sound like utter fools. That is exactly what we end up doing, when we begin finding our own 'scriptures', our own God, and our own Ten Commandments as answers to the criticisms of Judaism, Christianity and Islam. We do not need a 'religion' of our 'own'; we need no 'Hinduism' as a religion, to find out what we are and who we are. If we insist on this transformation, know this for certain: you will have to say that most Indians and your ancestors were exactly the kind of morons of modernity that Sir Babington Macaulay described not so long ago.

TRADITION AND RELIGION

There is also an additional element to this. To use the notion of 'truth' to characterize traditional practices is to commit the fallacy of a *category mistake*. The one intelligible notion of 'truth' we have today, makes truth into a property of sentences, that is, into a linguistic property. This is better called the 'philosophical' conception of truth instead of the 'Aristotelian conception of truth', where the notion of truth is defined entirely in terms of the accuracy or correctness of descriptions. Here, 'truth' and 'falsity' are seen as properties of natural language sentences or of propositions. It is only *of sentences* that we can say whether they are true or false. Even though we do use the notion of truth in multiple other ways, as when we say of someone that 'he is a true friend' or when we say 'only truth is the real' we are partially incapable (today) of fleshing out these other notions of truth. In this sense, we can use the predicate 'true' with respect to the linguistic descriptions of practices, but we cannot apply it to the practices themselves. While it might or might not be true to say that I wrote this piece on a computer, it is a category mistake to ascribe the predicate 'true' to the act of typing on a computer. The act of typing itself is neither true nor false. As human practices, traditions are neither true nor false, whereas some descriptions of such practices could be either true or false.

There is another question, which I have not taken up: *how sensible is it to speak even of Judaism, Christianity and Islam as 'religions'?* If the academic reflections about the use of this word teach us that it is suspect, what is its effect on the distinction I have drawn between 'religions' and 'traditions'? *Is this distinction more apparent than real?*

Given the focus of this chapter, my answer to these questions will be very brief. Let me begin with the second question.

The pioneering work of Cantwell Smith (*The Meaning and End of Religion*, 1962, London: SPCK) has had a major impact on the study of religion. Many people have begun to argue that the concept 'religion' needs to be thrown out because instead of helping us it merely hinders. There are merits to this suggestion. Insofar as a concept has pernicious effects on building a theory, it is better to get rid of it sooner rather than later. But even if we get rid of the concept, the object of our study remains. By not using the word 'cancer', or even rejecting the concept, we will not make the disease in question any less malignant or, if you prefer, any more benign. Of course, I am not implying that Cantwell Smith's suggestion amounts to a mere linguistic reform. But I do want to argue that the questions we confront while studying religion are not spurious but genuine, and the absence of obvious answers warrants further enquiries. Our problems persist irrespective of whether we use 'faith', 'cumulative tradition', 'religion', or whatever else to designate the phenomenon that we are investigating. I do believe that words like 'Christianity', 'Judaism' and 'Islam' refer to phenomena in the world. I advance no further claims about the nature of the phenomena: whether they are unitary, monolithic, or whatever else. These issues need to be settled by means of scientific enquiry and not by philosophical fiats.

By the same token, I do believe that there are important differences between phenomena like the above and the Indian traditions. These differences make a difference to how we study both. We can either study them the way they have been studied these past few centuries, which has not done much to advance our knowledge or try a different approach. I would like to try a different track.

SOME REMARKS

Both colonial and contemporary Western descriptions of India and her traditions transform Indians into something worse than children: they become the mental retards of modernity.

No amount of symbolic interpretation can take away the sting from the facts that one interprets: Indians worship the phallus, the cow, the monkey, the idol, and the naked fakir. We cannot instil pride in our children about their culture and traditions by telling them that these are all manifestations of Brahman. If you try talking that way with them, you will not be able to answer their question, "why not worship Brahman directly without having to worship all these other strange things?" without making your ancestors and the rest of the Indians look like fools. Make them first understand that these questions have their roots in the Semitic religions and the contempt these religions have for the Indian traditions. Tell them subsequently that it is their task to figure out what *'puja'* is, because it is not 'worship'. Of course, this requires honesty on our part: can we tell our children that we ourselves have failed in making sense of our traditions in the last few centuries and decades? Or, to save face, will we take recourse to feeding them with pseudo-answers about 'Hinduism', a 'religion', which supposedly hides profound and sublime truths? Only time will tell whether we can face the problems we confront or stick our heads in the sand hoping that they will go away.

CHAPTER 14

WHY UNDERSTAND WESTERN CULTURE?

If we want to be relevant and rational, we must not forget that we live in a world that does not merely include colonialism but also our responses to it. Our generation is formed (mostly) by a colonial past that has basically been accessed only through its critique – whether nationalist, Marxist, or Orientalist. Consequently, our questions and misgivings are different from those of a generation or two ago.

While it is true that our relationship to our own intellectual traditions is problematic, it is not clear what the nature of this problem is. We have had any number of pundits well-versed in Sanskrit literature, linguistics, and philosophy, but it has not helped us go any further, either as a nation or as a people. We have our share of intelligent men and women who have their feet planted both in Western and Indian culture; but we have hardly produced social theories of any merit and value. We have had, and continue to have, more than our share of nationalist, Marxist, and Orientalist 'thinkers', who reproduce time-worn criticisms of Western culture; but it has not made a difference to our intellectual traditions. Surely, if the problem was merely one of how we are related to our cultural traditions, it would have been solved by any of the above groups. Not only have they failed, but we are still in the dark about what bugs us about this situation. A back-to-the-roots movement is just as silly today as performing the routine of the brown Saheb and his butler-English.

Neither a D.D. Kosambi nor a Romila Thapar is able to specify what our problems are; it is important to realize that neither a Ronald Inden nor a Partha Chatterjee can do that either. Today's young readers will ask "who are these people?" and that is exactly the point. These were the intellectuals of the last few decades who have now faded into irrelevance. How then could a Patanjali or a Buddha or a Shankara be relevant? It might help in a vague way to discover that Patanjali devised a meta-language or that we were well on our way to discovering predicate calculus some four thousand years before the West discovered it. But how do such realizations help us in finding out what we must do today? It may be a fancy thing to speak of Edward Said or Jacques Derrida or to speak the language of post-colonial identity politics, but this is just a way for some Indians to make a living in the USA, and their talk is even less relevant than what the Buddha said about *atman* and *anatman*. We reproduce both our bondage to the West and our obliviousness to that bondage, whenever we reproduce the so-called social sciences or their critique.

The first prerequisite to break free from this bondage is to give up the complacent and smug belief that we know and understand Western culture and that we only need to understand ours better. We know little about the West or its culture. Let us try and describe the West as it *appears to us*, against the background of our culture, without reproducing the theories and descriptions of Western intellectuals. Very soon, we will discover that we know little about this culture; and that our ignorance here is every bit as profound and deep as our ignorance of our own culture.

We are a culture that does *puja* to Saraswathi – the embodiment of knowledge and learning. Yet, regarding knowledge about the world and people, we show appalling ignorance combined with mindboggling pretention. If there is a single pernicious impact that colonialism has had upon us (and there are many), it is to make us believe that we know the West. The truth is, we do not. When we begin to understand the West, only then will we begin to relate fruitfully and productively to our traditions.

The thing to keep in mind about our intellectual development, historically speaking, is that most of what we have learnt about ourselves has been the result of what has been said about us by the West. We relate to our own traditions and our own culture the way the West has understood them.

We have learnt that '*puja*' means worship; '*devas*' are 'gods'; '*atman*' is 'Self' (not to be confused with the empirical 'self'); 'Hinduism', 'Buddhism', 'Jainism', 'Saivism', etc. are 'religions'; '*sadhus*' are our 'holy' men or even our 'god-men'; '*tapas*' means doing 'penance'; and so on and so forth. This list is virtually endless. As we grow up and discover that there is *ayudha puja, go-puja* and *linga-puja*, either we are embarrassed to discover their English equivalents or insist that we do not *really* worship our work instruments, or cows or the phallus. We routinely translate 'idolatry' as '*murthi puja*' but insist that people do not *really* worship these images but merely... merely, what? The idea that one does not worship these 'images' but looks at them as 'symbols of Divinity' is an old Catholic argument that attempted to explain that they did not worship images. We think we are being 'clever' when we reinvent the wheel.

This raises the question: what are our people doing when they do *puja*? Are they worshipping or not? If it is not worship, what else are they doing when they do *puja*?

The point is this: most of us have learnt English through the mediation of our local languages. However, we did not establish the equivalence between these words based on our knowledge of phenomena like 'worship', 'God', 'religion', etc. We have merely been taught that they are equivalents of *puja, devata, dharma*, and so on. This is not a question of translation or of finding the right words from our languages to translate English (or any other European language). Rather it is one of understanding what these English words mean. And we can do so not by consulting the Oxford English Dictionary but by understanding the nature of religion. When we do this, we will begin to study and (partially) understand Western culture.

Why do we need to do this? Why not simply use words from our language and be done with it? Because this does not address the problem, let alone solve it. Consider one of the ideas that surfaces and resurfaces again and again: 'Hindutva' and 'Hindu fundamentalism'. These issues have been preoccupying Indian intellectuals and the Indian polity for quite a while now. We simply assume that 'Hinduism' exists, that it is a religion, that we too have 'fundamentalists' and 'secularists', etc. Here are some simple counter-questions: does Hinduism exist? If it does, is it a religion? What is religion so that we might say we too have it? These are not the sort of issues that can be solved by giving correct *definitions* but those that call for serious scientific investigation. If people find these questions ridiculous or insulting, my point is proved: we simply *assume* answers to them; we might even find, perhaps, that raising them is vaguely offensive. And that point is: these questions and the answers we have are the answers provided by Western culture. These are answers that the West came up with in their attempts to understand a culture different from their own.

In short, we do not have *access* to our own traditions in any direct fashion. We rely upon an understanding determined by the *Western* understanding of our traditions. Look at the Indian philosophical writing of the previous century to understand how deep this influence is. But we do not understand Western culture either, except by repeating what they have said about themselves. Here are some of their common themes we repeat: Western societies are democracies where the rule of Law prevails; either the People or the Parliament is the Sovereign; the Enlightenment brought forth the 'age of reason' which was critical about the role of religion in society; etc. Now, how much of what we know about ourselves is due to our own culture and how much of it is an ill-understood and ill-digested reproduction of the claims that Western culture makes about itself?

Are Shankara and the Buddha relevant to us today? The problems that Buddha and Shankara tried to solve, whatever they might have been, are not ours; hence their answers cannot be ours either, unless we assume that their questions and answers are timeless and universally valid. *If we assume this*, then we are compelled to admit that they *did not* produce knowledge. We do not have a single example of a knowledge that is timeless. Knowledge always develops and changes. The Bible, an example of a timeless and universally valid set of claims, is not knowledge. According to the believers, it is *the truth*. It is 'the truth' because it is God's revelation, and He is eternal and the truth. To claim that Buddha or Shankara produced eternal truths of this kind is silly to the extreme. If Buddha or Shankara produced knowledge, then that knowledge has to be made accessible for us in the 21st century. Thus, what we need to do is to formulate our own questions first and then see whether their solutions help *us* in our quest. It might be the case that they help someone in some place in the world today. I do not doubt this. The Gita, the Buddha or Shankara comfort me and bring solace in my dark moments as well. But this is not the issue. The issue is: how and why do they appear to help us? How to understand, to give but one example, that the world is *maya* or illusion? Am I to say that the world described by the natural sciences does not exist, or that my daily experience is an illusion? If not, what are they talking about? Surely, the issues are of this nature and not ones to take offence to.

That is why we need to understand Western culture. This is not Eurocentrism in any sense of the term. We need to do it, as I said, *against the background of our own culture*. How does the West appear to us? How do we appear to ourselves? These two questions are deceptively simple in their appearance. But simple, they certainly are not. We desperately *need* to understand Western culture, not by repeating what its intellectuals have said about itself but by studying it. We need to do this because our relation to ourselves and our past is determined by what the West has said about both.

CHAPTER 15

DISCRIMINATION OR CHOICE?

Take the issue of entry into the Shabarimala Temple as an example. It is used by many people as evidence of the discriminatory nature of the Indian traditions. Indians, we have been told, constantly discriminate and this is embedded in their immoral and unjust system called the 'caste system'. In its turn, this system is allegedly founded on 'Hinduism', the religion of the Hindus. Since this is important to the story about the 'immorality' of Indian society, let us look at 'discrimination' closely.

As mentioned earlier, I was once invited for a visit to the Swami Narayan Temple (BAPS) to talk to some of their Sadhus. These Sadhus practice strict avoidance of women of eight different types. It is called Ashtanga Brahmacharya. Because of this, the Sadhus would not have women present at the meeting. Women, however, were otherwise welcome to visit the temple. As I recall, my female students were upset and indignant by this exclusion and felt *discriminated against*. A few years later, one of my teachers from Belgium visited another wing of the Swami Narayan group and also found that women were 'discriminated against' because they were not allowed to go the full distance into the temple when the Sadhus were present. In both cases, I was puzzled by their reaction. I explained that the action of the Sadhus had nothing to with discrimination against women but expressed the strict Brahmacharya vows they practiced instead. The question here is: why did my students and my teacher experience discrimination, whereas I saw none and knew that none was intended?

Consider another example. Once I had the occasion to read some pages of a book called *The Language of the Gods in the World of Men* by Sheldon Pollock together with a few people in India. The book is about the role of Sanskrit among other things in Indian culture. Pollock talks about Sanskrit in Ancient India in these terms: because Sanskrit was used primarily in the context of rituals during its early days, its role was both limited and exclusive. It was limited in the sense that it was used primarily in *Vaidika* practices and exclusive in the sense that only a few could speak Sanskrit, while most were forbidden from learning it. Of course, there is no shred of evidence that people were forbidden from using Sanskrit for purposes other than ritual performances. Nor is there evidence that groups of people were forbidden from learning Sanskrit or that teachers were not allowed to teach this language to others. One can reasonably assume, however, that many people did not speak or understand Sanskrit. This 'sacerdotal isolation' (Pollock's words) of Sanskrit, indicated both its limited and exclusive nature. He believes that this is inequality and that it expresses discrimination in Ancient India.

There is a puzzle here. How does Pollock know that there was discrimination when there is no evidence for it? Consider the language I speak at home: Sankethi. Only those born into the Sankethi community learn this language and one does not teach this language to other people. Does it follow from this that, *therefore*, we discriminate against other peoples and groups in India? In fact, most people in India have not heard of Sankethi and see no reason to learn this language. So, if a group develops a language for some purpose and does not teach it to others in the world, does it indicate discrimination? Why can one not develop a language (like Sankethi was developed) for use by a restricted number of people?

What is discriminatory about it? The only possible way to speak of discrimination in this case is by assuming that languages ought to be universally accessible and one ought to teach everyone every possible language. But what if people do not want to learn? Could one say that in Ancient India very few people were interested in learning Sanskrit and most were not? If not, why not?

Common to both these examples is their 'normative' assumption. The first assumes that the Sadhus ought to be accessible to all and if they are not, they discriminate. The temple 'ought' to be accessible not only to all but it also 'ought' to be so under all circumstances. Any restriction here is seen as discrimination. Equally, in the second example, the assumption is that every language ought to be accessible to all people, always and under all circumstances. More generally put, the idea is that everything ought always to be accessible to all people under all circumstances. Such a normative assumption is ridiculous, of course. No one claims that my wife or my house should always be accessible to all people in all circumstances. In other words, the notion of discrimination is very *plastic,* and it is used as it suits the prejudices of individuals.

Consider another aspect of so-called caste discrimination – marriage within one's own caste ('savarna' marriage). If a Brahmin seeks a Brahmin spouse by refusing to marry outside his caste, this is alleged to indicate caste discrimination. What is discriminatory about this? The only possible argument is that the 'search space' for finding a spouse ought not to be restricted. The claim is that one 'ought' to search everywhere and that if you search only in one 'space' then you are discriminating against other 'spaces'. This is silly. No one can search everywhere at the same time; one can only search in some specific space. Does it mean that because you search in one specific space you are discriminating against other places? In fact, in scientific research, a problem is well-structured if and only if it restricts the search space: the narrower the search space, the better is the problem formulation. So, what is discriminatory about this? Only the normative assumption that one 'ought' to search everywhere and one 'ought' to marry wherever one finds a possible spouse can lead one to think this way. Surely you cannot get more foolish than this. What if I want to marry a Brahmin? What if this is my preference? What is wrong with this? A normative assumption leads to the denial of personal preferences in marriage and imposes an obligation – an 'ought'. (But if you marry one, you cannot marry all other women. By this logic, surely, this is also discrimination?)

The point is this: if I want to marry within one community, it does not follow that, therefore, I am discriminating against other communities. If some people speak some language or another, and only they do so, it does not follow, that, therefore, they are discriminating against all other people. If the Sadhus practice Brahmacharya, it does not follow, therefore, that they are discriminating against women. In each of these cases, they choose one option, and this does not discriminate against others. Only a silly normative assumption can transform this behaviour into a discriminatory act.

Of course, those who see discrimination in this are quick to shift grounds to point out cases of violence among those who do marry peoples from other 'castes'. Now they say they are being ill-treated, beaten or killed by 'high caste' families. Again, this is no explanation for discrimination. The violence is heinous, but this does not mean that it is because of caste discrimination.

Consider now the oft-used hypothetical situations where persons are denied medical treatment or a job opportunity on grounds of caste.

In the first place, I have not heard of people being turned away from a doctor or a hospital in India on grounds of their *jati*. On the other hand, I have heard of any number of cases in the U.S.

(see Michael Moore's brilliant documentary *Sicko* on the American Health Care System), where people are turned away from hospitals or denied medical treatment because they do not have the right insurance policy. Many have died too because of that. Yet, we do not speak of discrimination of any kind present in the U.S. culture in these cases but speak only of the rotten health care system that the U.S. has. However, we would not hesitate to convict Indian culture or 'Hinduism' of caste discrimination, if any such incident were to occur in India.

In the second place, even if we were to assume that people are turned away from a hospital or denied medical treatment because of their *jati*, I am not sure what makes this into *caste discrimination*. If the hospital is established with the explicit goal of helping everyone unconditionally and the doctor has sworn the Hippocratic oath of helping everyone who asks for his help, then, turning a suffering human being away on grounds of their *jati* is a violation of this oath. Even here, it is either the hospital or the doctor who are guilty. However, they are guilty of violating either the stated goal or the sworn oath. This does not make it an instance of caste discrimination but one of violating explicit goals and oaths.

When a hospital is meant to treat all the citizens of India and refuses to treat some of them because of other considerations that are non-technical in nature, such a hospital is violating legal requirements. If these legal requirements are also moral in nature (this requires additional moral assumptions), then, and only then, could we speak of them as also being morally discriminatory.

The same consideration applies to job opportunities. If an institution offers a job opportunity with the explicit claim that no other conditions apply for success except, say, academic qualifications and despite this, chooses less qualified people on grounds of their *jati* then, yes, there is discrimination on the basis of 'caste'. However, when being born in a *jati* is considered enough of a qualification or if a college run by a religious institution chooses people based on their religious leanings, what kind of discrimination are we talking about?

Just because someone is denied access to some service based on caste, that alone is not sufficient to transform such an act into a discriminatory act. It becomes that only when the explicitly stated condition allows everyone who satisfies said condition to have access to that service and yet denies access to that service to someone on some other unstated ground.

One might find it objectionable to exclude people on grounds of their birth. I would like to suggest that such an exclusion becomes a case of discrimination if, and only if, an additional normative assumption is present.

Consider the presence of all kinds of youth hostels in India that cater only to students from specific *jatis*: Kuruba hostel, Gowda hostel, Lingayata hostels, and such. Is this exclusion also a case of discrimination? If these are legitimate institutions, then exclusion based on birth is not enough to speak of discrimination. One speaks of dining practices in some temples and insists that exclusion based on birth is not acceptable, while at the same time one has no qualms about excluding people based on money and power (like from a club membership).

If we look at it empirically, we will find that it is far more difficult to become rich or powerful (if one is born poor or powerless) than it is to enter these dining halls in temples. All one needs to do is to wear the 'sacred thread', claim to be a second-generation immigrant from Rajasthan or Bihar or some far-off place and mention some fictitious sub-*jati* as an 'upper caste' or Brahmanical *jati*. In other words, one must wear a thread and tell a lie. Which is easier? To tell a lie or to cough up Rs. 10,000 when you are poor? Nothing is easier in India today than changing *jatis*, even at an official level. Consider how many people routinely obtain false *jati* certificates by paying a bribe to the concerned officials!

Before we talk about caste discrimination, it would be wise if we reflect on which normative assumptions are involved in such judgments and whether they are reasonable and defensible. Not every alleged case of so-called caste discrimination is also a case of caste discrimination. Simply reproducing the commonly held criticisms of the Indian 'caste system' will not do. There is much that requires doing before one can come up with a coherent message that political parties can transmit.

Let's say you believe that the Brahmacharya of the Sadhus at the Swami Narayan Temple is all rubbish. Now, of course, their beliefs about Brahmacharya and women might be *your* reason to rubbish their beliefs, but you cannot deny their freedom to believe in their 'rubbish' and practice it for themselves. There is nothing morally wrong in having wrong or false beliefs. Atheists, for instance, genuinely believe that religion is dangerous for human beings but that does not mean, therefore, that people should be forbidden from being believers. The men and women (yes, women too) who are followers of Swami Narayan in fact share the belief of the Sadhus. These women do not protest that they are not allowed to enter the temples in the presence of the Sadhus. In fact, if they happen to visit the temple when the Sadhus are also there, they respectfully wait at some distance and enter only during the hours when the Sadhus are not supposed to be there. They do not feel discriminated against.

The reason why my Belgian students felt discriminated against lies elsewhere, namely, in the normative assumptions they make and not in the beliefs and practices of the Sadhus. This becomes obvious when you realize that the men and women who follow this tradition also share the beliefs and practices of the Sadhus. I have known wonderful men, who practiced extremely strict Brahmacharya because they were *bhaktas* of Anjaneya or Hanumantha. As you know, Anjaneya is a very great *bhakta* of Rama and a strict Brahmachari. Even if these Sadhus are wrong about their ideas and practices, one cannot say, therefore, they are morally wrong. Much in the same way that the women do not come into the temple when the Sadhus are present, the Sadhus are not allowed to come into the temple during certain hours of the day. In this sense, the restrictions boil down to this: women do not enter the temple during certain hours and the Sadhus do not enter during certain other hours. Even if the temple is a public space, whatever the word 'public' might mean in this context, I do not see what makes this restriction immoral.

All I want to suggest is that we can view some act as morally discriminatory if, and only if, we make some moral assumptions in our arguments. Similarly, *we need to add moral assumptions when we speak of caste discrimination.*

Let's look at another example I was once given: Rajesh and Pinky, two youngsters, commit suicide. They were in love, but because Rajesh was a 'Dalit' and Pinky was a 'savarna', her parents did not consent to their marriage. They died in each other arms near the railway tracks, after consuming poison.

Some responses are in order, if at least to bring out a *tacit assumption* here. We know the story of Romeo and Juliet, both of whom died because their feuding families did not consent to their marriage. Should the state intervene between all *feuding* families because in some cases it leads to tragedies like Romeo and Juliet? Where is the difference between this case and that of Rajesh and Pinky? You might want to say that a feud between families is a personal or a family matter, whereas caste discrimination is a social one. But this is merely an *assumption*, which has taken on the status of a fact to us. Why do we not see this as a 'personal' or a familial matter as well — a matter that involves the notions of Rajesh's and

Pinky's parents? Here's an example from my own personal story. My uncle was a rigid orthodox Brahmin. His own daughter, my niece, married a Dalit with his blessings; I am married to a Belgian woman (who eats both beef and pork and was a Christian) but my side of the family raised no problems.

What does this anecdote indicate? How 'tolerant' my family is? Or the fact that there are no social rules that *all* Brahmins *must* follow? The story of Pinky and Rajesh is an instance of social injustice, if and only if, one assumes that it is *social* injustice. Such reasoning is another instance of the fallacy called *petitio principii*, i.e., assuming the truth of what needs to be proved to be true. That the so-called caste system is causally responsible for ills in India requires *showing* and demonstrating not merely assuming. Nehruvian socialism *assumes* this missionary hallucination as a truth about Indian society. Modern-day common sense does the same. This prevents us from understanding and solving the many problems that we confront in our society. Misdiagnosing a patient will not cure the disease. We do this all the time while busy parroting the Western story about the immoral caste system.

CHAPTER 16

A DIALOGUE WITH AN INDOLOGIST

Imagine that someone, let us say she is an American Indologist, comes along and sees me doing 'something' and asks what I am doing. I say, "I am doing *puja* to Shiva." As a result, let us say that a conversation begins between the two of us. From here on, we can follow two possible threads. The first thread goes like this.

(1) When she asks why I do it, I say, "it is our tradition, or that I am a *Bhakta* of Shiva, or because my mother said I should", or whatever else happens to be the case. If she asks me why Shiva has the form he has, either I tell her the story from the Puranas or provide her a *sthalapurana*, a story about a particular temple. Or I simply say, "this is how we do it."

1.1. Let us say, she pursues the story from the Puranas and asks me "So, you are worshipping the Lingam of Shiva?" I say, "yes, indeed, this *is* the Shiva Lingam." Being persistent, she goes further: "do you know what 'Lingam' means?" I reply "well, yes, I do know some of its meanings as we use it in our language."

1.2. She asks what '*puja*' is and what 'lingam' means in English. Here is what I would say *today*: "*Puja* is best understood as a ritual; as far as 'Lingam' is concerned, I suggest you see it as 'the form' in which this ritual is performed."

1.3. She says, "So, you think that Lingam is a symbol for Shiva. Then, you must also acknowledge that modern research has shown that it is a fertility symbol that many ancient cults also used."

I smile and say *today*: "The Lingam is not a symbol; nor do we need to appeal to modern research or speak about symbolisms to speak of our deities. In fact, what you are proposing is an age-old Christian doctrine. You see, seeing the Cross or an icon as a symbol for the divinity and as something that 'simple minds' need to understand 'God' is a millennium-old doctrine that a Catholic pope propounded. He did it to say that the simple Christian folk did not worship idols but needed that symbol to worship God. You see, he and the flock that he was tending believe that God is outside the Cosmos and is outside space-time. Thus, there is a need to symbolize this transcendent being in the here and now. Your 'modern' research thus turns out to be an old Christian claim. In contrast, Indians do not see the Lingam as the symbol of Shiva. This *para-devata* is in the *apara* (in the *Iha*, in the *Vishwa*). That is, the Lingam, an object in the *apara* is how the *para* (in our case, Shiva) manifests or is present in the world. *The Lingam is Shiva. It is not a symbol but the form in which Shiva is present in the apara.*"

(2) She asks, "why does Shiva have this form?" Because I am not trying to be polemical, I tell her our stories from the Puranas and say it is one of the stories from our tradition. And I add, "to perform puja to Shiva *means* to perform the ritual to this form." Because my description has the form of a definition (Shiva puja = ritual to this form) no sensible discussion about my practice is possible.

Let us now suppose that she contests my characterization of *puja* as a ritual and the fact that Lingam refers to the form in which Shiva *puja* is done.

(3) "You are wrong. *Puja* is 'worship' and 'lingam' means 'phallus'. Therefore, you are 'worshipping the phallus' when you say that you are doing *puja* to the Shiva Lingam" she responds.

Here is what I would say *today*: "You see, the English word 'worship' basically comes from theology where one worships either

God or the Devil. No interpretation of such a theology allows us to consider Shiva as 'God'. This leaves us with the only possibility that Shiva is the Devil or one of his minions. Is this what you want to ask: why we worship the Devil or one of his minions? In that case, this discussion is not about the meaning of words but about the truth of Christian theology."

Either she denies this conclusion or asks for further explications. Let us take up her denial first.

(3.1.) "No, that is not what 'worship' means. The word means 'reverence'. I am not a Christian; I am a Jew; I know very little of Christian theology even though I was married to a Christian for some time."

I would say the following *today*: "I would be willing to accept your definition of 'worship'. But if I do, I must do violence to other people and cultures: the Jewish, the Christian and the Muslim. In all these cultures, one can show 'reverence' to the elderly, to the king, to the powerful, etc. To say that someone shows reverence to God in the same way they show reverence to these other entities is to transform all of them into idolaters, which, according to their theologies, is the greatest sin of all. From your definition, it would follow that they are not worshipping God at all, if all they show is 'reverence' the same as they accord to any political functionary! I am sorry, but the translation of *'puja'* cannot be a mere linguistic issue without it raising theological questions."

(3.2.) Let us say she asks for an explication and says the following: "Sanskrit-English dictionaries and Indian Sanskrit teachers who know English, translate *'puja'* as 'worship'. Are you saying their knowledge of either of the languages is deficient and that *you are the only one* who knows how to translate *'puja'* correctly?"

Being a reasonable person, I would not get offended by her rhetorical attempts to make me appear ridiculous. I would say the following *today*: "You see, we learnt English through Indian languages and were taught that *puja* means 'worship'. We gave the meaning of '*puja*' to the English word 'worship'. The first generations of translators decided to translate *puja* as worship because they were convinced that we are idolaters and worshipped the Devil. So, you see, we must discuss historical issues about colonialism and what it means to a culture like ours to resolve the issues of translation. Shall we begin with that discussion?"

Thus, I can sketch several other scenarios of the possible conversational moves open to this person. A few reflections about this conversation are in order because it is very important to realize what has happened consistently throughout.

(A) The first thing to notice is that, in all these scenarios, I am *defining* the terms of the debate. She is unable to do this with respect to what *I am doing*.

(B) I can do it *because* I am knowledgeable about Western culture. That is, I am not ignorant of Western culture the way I was when I was 14 or 24. Therefore, I am able to tell her *today* that she does not understand her own culture as well as I understand hers.

(C) My principle of charity forbids me from transforming any culture, whether hers or mine, into a bunch of idiots. My conversational move in (3.1) makes me *defend* the Jewish, Islamic, and Christian cultures because of this principle. Of course, the same principle makes me defend Indian traditions as reasonable ones too.

(D) I am not making use of any fancy defensive 'explanation', symbolic explanation, or any explanation that many Indians come up with to defend their traditions. Such 'explanations' arise out of ignorance: both of their own traditions and, above all, of Western culture. They have little understanding of the subjects they talk about, but their conviction is that they know what is there to know.

Most English-speaking Indians I have met are pompous and empty: they argue for the sake of arguing and believe that knowledge is a matter of providing citations and references to books. But they have no understanding of either their own traditions or that of the West. These are our 'intellectuals'.

Who would have thought that to understand my mother, I need to understand my mother-in-law? What you see in my imaginary conversation with this American is this realization. We need to breed a new set of intellectuals. They will have to take a different route than the one pursued so far.

CHAPTER 17

WORDS AND THEIR CONSEQUENCES

In this chapter, I will take up three examples where we keep parroting European descriptions of the world without having any understanding of Western culture. You will see how the world of European experience has generated our descriptions of India. It is popular in some circles to speak of untranslatable Indian or Sanskrit words, but the more urgent question is: do you know what you are saying when you speak in English?

I

IDOL WORSHIP

Take two common sense ideas: (i) Indians worship idols and (ii) the slogan, *'murthi puja is a mahapaapa'*.

Let me begin with a question I was once asked: "Is there anything intrinsically wrong in performing idol worship in the way something is intrinsically wrong with robbery?"

Let's assume that we are clear what robbery is and that it is intrinsically wrong. We need to make these assumptions because (a) in all probability, the robbers do not see anything intrinsically wrong in robbing; (b) some of us might not be willing to call a Robin Hood who robs only the rich and passes most of the spoils to the poor, an immoral person; (c) it is unclear whether the windfall profits that big corporations have made in the last decades constitute robbery or not. Under these assumptions, we are drawing an analogy between idol worship and an act of a human being towards fellow human beings. This analogy breaks down because idol worship is not a relation between human beings but between an act of a human being and an inanimate entity that an idol is.

However, one can look at 'morality' as obedience to God's will in the sense that our moral laws are His commandments. When looked at this way then, yes, idol worship is intrinsically wrong because in doing so one disobeys God's will. In Christianity, immorality or sin is the act of disobeying God. And He has forbidden worshipping Him as an idol. Not only has God forbidden idol worship but He has also revealed how He should be worshipped. Each Semitic religion tells its own story about the 'how' of worship. You might want to argue that there are no harmful consequences from idol worship even in such a situation. However, you would be wrong. Through false worship, you condemn yourself to damnation for all eternity. This is the fundamental freedom that God has given to human beings – to choose between Him, the possibility of salvation and eternal life on the one hand, and false gods, the Devil, false worship, and eternal damnation on the other. In this sense, idol worship has a clear meaning and reference. It is a clearly defined concept in the theologies of the Semitic religions.

Now, you could strip the concept of 'idol-worship' of its meaning and reference and use an empty word that refers to the Indian act of doing *puja*, say, in a temple. You might use the English word 'worship' to refer to the act of doing *puja* or even to *upaasana*. Furthermore, *murthi* or *vigraha* can be replaced by the word 'idol'. And you can use the word *paapa* or *mahapaapa* in place of 'sin'. Now the question about idol worship becomes: "Is *murthi puja a mahapaapa?*" Because of the word-replacements we just performed, you believe this is the same as asking: "Is idol worship a sin?"

Notice, however, what you are doing. You presuppose that your audience is at home with Indian practices, knows what you are talking about, and understands your account. But the question is this: are you speaking the English language or not? Even though you use English words, you are not speaking English. Any string of empty syllables could be employed to do the same job English words are doing in this context. Suppose that I say *puja* should be replaced by 'pif'; *paapa* should be replaced by 'paf'; 'idol' should be replaced by 'poof', I would get the same result: Is poof-pif also a paf?

The illusion that you are saying and doing something intelligible arises from our history. We are taught that *puja* is 'worship', *murthi* is 'idol', and *paapa* is 'sin'. Notice, however, that in the act of translation, you are establishing equivalence in meaning between these words. That is why we call this a translation and not just an arbitrary replacement of words. Those who undertook these translations did believe that Indians worshipped idols, cows, rats and so on. They established these conventions and none of the Indian intellectuals, whether of yesteryears or contemporaneous, protested. They perpetuated and sustained these conventions, all the while believing that they understand the meaning and reference of these words in the English language. The problem does not lie in their lack of understanding of English *but in their lack of understanding of Western culture.* We have no clue about the extent to which Semitic theologies have made a home for themselves in linguistic practices.

This problem of not understanding Western culture while genuinely believing that we do is compounded when we account for religions like Christianity using *our* own intellectual frameworks. While it stands to reason that we would try to understand another culture within the framework of our own, our abysmal ignorance of the West creates formidable problems. We cannot look at Semitic religions as human expressions and human creations. In this framework, we cannot even begin to understand what they say about themselves, namely, that they are not human creations but the revelations of God. I have read people who write that 'Hinduism' also speaks of revelation: '*apaurusheya*' means that the Veda is a 'revelation of God', they claim. As much as the Semitic religions did not understand the Indian traditions, we too do not understand their religions. This is the 'blindness' of the heathen that I talk about. We fail to see their religions for what they are when seeing them as human traditions instead. There is something defensible and indefensible in this. It is defensible when we try to understand religions; but becomes indefensible when we do so without learning anything about them in the first place.

Finally, I would like to draw your attention to our language use. I do not know when the word '*murthi-puja*' was coined. But I do vaguely remember reading that Raja Ram Mohun Roy gave currency to this word by saying that it was a *maha-paapa*. While writing this chapter, it struck me that our language use is nuanced. Rarely, if ever, do we say that we did *puja* to the *murthi* of Ganesha, when we go to the temples. We say that we did *puja* to Ganesha. Hardly, if ever, do we use *vigraha* in this context. When we use words like *murthi* or *vigraha*, we refer to statues. We say things like "the *murthi* was 50 feet tall"; "in this or that temple, the *vigraha* is very beautiful", and so on. We use these words only when we refer to human creations and physical objects. I hardly recollect anyone saying that "I did *puja* to the Ganesha *murthi* in that temple." They say, instead that they did *puja* to Ganesha in that temple. If this recollection of mine is also true of how we normally use these words, then, it appears that we hardly speak of '*murthi* puja', let alone do it. The question "to whom did you do puja"?' never elicits the answer: "I did puja to the *murthi* of Ganesha in that temple."

If you were to ask 100 knowledgeable Indians about the *puja* of Ganesha, you are likely to get as many different answers, which are all satisfactory in some sense or another. This is in stark contrast to the sorts of answers that you would get if you were to ask 100 knowledgeable Christians about the Catholic Mass. There are strict limits on what the Mass could be said to mean to a believer. These limits are set by Christian theology, whether Catholic or Protestant. The *puja* of Ganesha does not set any such limits to the person who does this *puja*. From this situation, you can go one of the two ways. One is what *appears* to us as the more familiar way: which of the answers is the right one? The second is to ask ourselves the questions: why do these answers appear acceptable to us? What do this question and its answers tell us about the Indian traditions? In other words, we should take the 'facts' from our culture as problems that require solutions.

Why do we want to do this? It is because how we understand our culture is thickly overlaid with what other cultures have told us about ourselves. Consequently, we misunderstand ourselves. We need to do research and yet more research to understand ourselves and the others.

II

POLYTHEISM

Consider the notion of 'polytheism' that anthropology of religion, practitioners of religious studies, and sociologists use and which has seeped into our everyday language use. In scholarly parlance as well as in our common sense, it is supposed to connote a multiplicity of 'gods' while monotheism is said to refer to a single 'God'. Do not miss the way these words are capitalized as well.

Now ask yourself this: what does it mean to speak of multiple gods?

It is to say that there is more than one God. There must be at least two. However, who or what is that God such that there might be more than one? To answer this question, if one refers to the meaning of this word, unsurprisingly it turns out, the dictionary meaning is also the meaning ascribed by the Semitic religions. Amongst other things, 'God' is the creator of the universe. If this is what God means, there cannot be more than one God. How can there be multiple creators of a Universe, when God refers to that being which created the Universe? How then to speak of polytheism? We can only do so if we assume that there is one God and that there are also other creatures in existence who claim the status of godhood. The claim of such creatures must be false because the very definition of God attributes this status to only one entity. Or there must be one God and many false gods who are different from and other than the True One. This is precisely what Semitic religions say: there is but one true God, and there are many false gods. A polytheist worships these false gods but not the True One. He is a heathen who worships the devil. This is what Christianity said of the Roman religions, of the Greek religions, and of the Indian 'religions'. How is it possible that the social sciences blithely take over the word 'polytheism' and use it without recognizing that it is senseless to do so without assuming the truth of Semitic theologies?

Within the (simplified) framework sketched above, this notion makes perfect sense theologically. The plurality of gods can only refer to entities other than God; there are many false gods and only one True God. If you take away this theological framework, the notion of polytheism becomes internally contradictory: if God is that being which created the world, and is thus the Lord of the Universe, how can there be a plurality of such entities? If a multiplicity exists, none of them is God. If none is God there can be no multiplicity of gods either. Therefore, polytheism is possible if and only if polytheism is impossible.

Here is why this arcane discussion is relevant to us. How many of us have not been taught and still teach that 'Hinduism' is a polytheistic (or a henotheistic) religion? To the European Christians, and their liberal secular counterparts, who continue to write books and treatises about Hindu polytheism, such appellations make perfect sense. They have not left their theological framework behind. But to us, people from another culture, this should not make sense. In fact, I suggest it does not. But we continue to act as though the notion of polytheism makes linguistic sense when it is perfect semantic nonsense. Why do we do this?

Partly, but only partly, because that is how we have learnt English: we were taught that '*deva*' was 'god', '*puja*' is 'worship' and so on. Who coined these terms? Well, people with a theologically inspired framework. To them, 'Hinduism', 'Buddhism', 'Jainism' were not only religions but also pagan or heathen religions, where the Devil and his minions were worshipped.

Consider some of the questions which ask 'Hindus' whether they 'worship' lingam, stones, monkeys, rats, and such like. First, it is important to realize that 'worship' is a theological concept – nothing like our notion of 'puja'. You can worship only 'God', in the same sense in which you can eat only what is food to you. It is possible that you worship false gods because they *deceive* you into worshipping them. This is what you do when you worship images created by human beings while assuming that you worship 'God'. This 'God' is not any Tom, Dick, or Harry, but The Perfect Being, The Creator, The Lord of the Universe. Again, ask yourself this simple question: which simpleton ever thought that some rat, a cow, a crow, or the stone lingam is 'The Perfect Being, The Creator, The Lord of the Universe'? Simpletons exist everywhere but if entire cultures and peoples from Asia to Africa comprised only of such people, their cultures could never have survived. Whatever the future might bring, India is a culture, and it has survived for a couple of thousand years. Are we to assume that Indians do not know they have physiological fathers and mothers, and that they were brought into being by a crow, a rat, or by the lingam made from stone?

In other words, we really need to re-think what we have been taught about who we are and what we do. Our question in this context should not be what *puja* means, or how it should be translated into English, but what is it we Indians do, when we do *puja*.

This applies not merely to the endless diatribes about 'Hinduism' and 'Buddhism', but to many other things that we have imbibed along with our mother's milk. It appears to me that some of us, living elsewhere, in another culture and at other times than our forefathers, can at least attempt to undertake the job of critically reflecting on our own experiences instead of reproducing barren third-rate ideas borrowed from second-hand sources far from our shores.

III

ABOUT 'GOD'

Here is a challenge: how would you translate the word 'God' into Sanskrit? Your answer must satisfy some minimum conditions because the question meets these conditions. Let me say clearly what these conditions are, so that transparent rules and an even playground favour no one party in the dispute.

Let us accept the best theory of meaning that exists in the marketplace. As far as I know, the book that plays this role most admirably, while satisfying the proponents of different theories of meaning expounded during the last century or so, is Prashant Parikh's *Language and Equilibrium* (MIT Press, 2010). His formal apparatus allows for the existence of 'word meanings' without sacrificing the idea that the meanings of sentences are context-dependent. It makes sense of statements such as "the meaning of red light is..." without restricting the application of 'meaning' to words and sentences alone.

The Indian cognate of the word 'God' must satisfy the use and meaning of the words *'theos'* and *'deus'*. This is an obvious condition because these Greek and Latin words are at the origin of the meaning of the English word 'God'.

The Sanskrit word you provide should be capable of being used sensibly in those contexts where 'God' has been used, primarily (a) by Catholic theologians in the last two millennia and (b) by the Protestant theologians since the Reformation. That is, the Sanskrit word should generate the same well-formed sentences, syntactically and semantically, that the word God produces. If it does not, obviously, it cannot be a cognate.

The Sanskrit word cannot have a purely stipulative meaning. That is, it cannot be a word with a technical meaning that an individual declares. Such a stipulation would be a part of some theory where a word has been 'defined' in a particular way. It must satisfy the condition that it has a 'word meaning', that is, it is well-known and used in the literature very frequently, the way 'God' is used in English.

This word must be used in the same sense as God as it is used by people of all persuasions over the course of the last two millennia. That is, (a) we must be able to make sense of, say, Shankara and Ramanuja using this Sanskrit equivalent for God the way we can use the word God to make sense of Thomas Aquinas and Martin Luther; (b) this word should make sense of the writings of these people. Simply suggesting that words like Ishvara, or Brahma do the job is an inadmissible move for the simple reason that this is what the dispute is about. This is what you need to prove and not just declare. Neither is an argument from authority (saying that thinker X or Y used it) acceptable because it is a fallacy in informal logic to use that as proof. We need arguments that are logically and linguistically consistent for proposing a Sanskrit equivalent.

I proposed what I have written above as a challenge on a forum that claims to specialize in the study of Religions in South Asia. None took up this challenge except a person who wrote that one should '*bolo ram ram*'.

Why does this question matter? What is the fuss about? Can we not just give an 'Indian meaning' to English words? No, we cannot. If 'Indian secularism' means something different from 'Western secularism', as our intellectuals claim, why cannot Indian 'God' mean something different from the Western 'God'?

The problem is not whether Indians can provide their own 'meanings' to words that differ from how the Oxford English Dictionary defines them. Nor does the problem have to do with being fair to speakers from different cultures and therefore adding their 'meanings' to words in the English language. There are two other issues here: one is about what words like 'God', 'temple', 'sacredness' mean in European languages; the other is about communicability and research.

Words like the above are theoretical terms in Christian theology. As such, they have also found their home in European natural languages. Thus, when one talks about religion, one uses these terms in a rather precise way even in the European natural languages. When we talk about 'atoms' or 'genes' in English, we make use of a part of their technical meanings from scientific theories. One rhetorical question could be: why can't Indians mean 'haircut' with the word 'atoms' and mean 'masala dosa' when they use 'genes?' They can; they have the freedom to do so. However, when they do so with others who follow the technical meanings of these words (as defined in these theories) even partially, Indians run the risk of being incoherent or downright stupid. This is not an issue of 'fairness' or 'freedom of speech'.

Let me generalize the above examples into the following claim: we cannot translate words like 'religion' or 'sacred' or 'norm' or 'rights' or 'sovereignty' or 'God', etc., because we lack their equivalents in our languages. That is, we do not understand English the way the British, the Americans, etc. understand English. However, unlike them – at least they say they do not understand many Indian words – we claim that we understand all their words, their culture, and their languages. They have an advantage over us: *they know that they do not know*. But we do not even know the extent or nature of our ignorance. We say that we understand their languages and culture without difficulty. Wow!

Of course, there is a reverse side to this problem. In the same way we fail to understand their languages and words, they too cannot 'translate' our words and, if they do, there is a failure in understanding. A favourite theme of some is that only insiders should study India and that foreigners should not do so because of this problem. We apparently have '*adhikara*' to study Sanskrit and our culture that Westerners do not have, because it is difficult if not impossible to translate many Sanskrit terms into English.

We know that actions have consequences. We must learn that words too have consequences.

CHAPTER 18

FROM SAMPRADAYA TO ADHIKARA: SOME DISTORTIONS

Our culture has not disintegrated. This means, *in principle*, that we can access our traditions. That is, it is possible for us to try and find out how the earlier generations either in fact accessed or could possibly have accessed their experiences. However, today, we access the Indian traditions the *way the West has taught us*: we access them through religious, philosophical, or poetic, literary, etc., texts. That is, we are not so much taught to access the Indian traditions as how we 'ought' to be accessing them – through texts. This is coupled with a strange relationship to practices, festivals, celebrations, etc. On the one hand many of us practice them enthusiastically; yet, on the other hand, we are willing to accept (and bend our heads down in shame) when the criticism that some of these practices are not 'founded' or 'justified' in our texts. "Why wear *kumkum* on our foreheads?"

When this type of question is asked, of men for example, some are embarrassed and wipe it off, while others come up with ad hoc explanations about the pharmacological interaction between *kumkum* and some nerve-endings in the brain. This 'explanation' is supposed to provide a scientific basis for this practice. Why this attempt? Because, without it, we think we come across as silly and stupid people. How can men wear *kumkum* on their foreheads or stick *Tulasi* leaves behind their right ear or…? This indicates that we believe that our practices need to be sanctioned by some or another theoretical justification. To put it a bit crudely, we believe that our practices must be 'textually' justified. Our defence of our traditions follows the same route. But what happens to *our traditions* when we access them as *texts*? What happens *to us* when we do so? I will take up these questions now.

Let us begin by noticing that we can access the past mainly through (a) texts and (b) artefacts. Their close connection is the primary reason why archaeology and history were united in a single department in European universities for a long time. While historians focussed basically on texts, archaeologists concentrated on human artefacts. In the West, for a long period, the Bible was considered to be the only historical text worth studying. It was not only considered to be true but was also known to be true (in the West). This text was a chronicle not only of the human past but also of what God intended for humankind. What did God intend for us? How could we faithfully follow his wishes? Answers to these questions were of supreme interest and crucial importance. Not knowing the answers to these questions got you a one-way ticket to Hell for all eternity. In other words, the faithful needed to know not only what God 'said' but also what he 'meant'. One could decipher God's 'intention' only by reading and interpreting His word. Thus, the Biblical sentences conveyed meanings and these expressed God's intention. Consequently, reading the Bible was the occupation of the clergy and they were expected to tell their flock what God ordained, wanted and thereby save their souls from eternal damnation.

The Protestant Reformation of the 16th century came and upset this apple cart. The Protestants asserted that every believer could read and understand the Bible unaided by the priests and the clergy. Each one of us had our special relationships with the Almighty and all of us could read, understand and 'divine' God's intention on Earth. The Catholics had failed to understand God's message; their interpretations of the Gospels were false and expressed the intentions of the hated priesthood. Because it is obvious that messages always express the intentions of the author, it became easy to characterize the intentions of the priests as unholy; like the world over, priests merely intend to oppress people and want to lead them to Hell. They were seduced by the Devil to perform his task on earth. This is what the Protestants believed.

It took a few centuries, but eventually this idea took very deep roots amongst the populace. Developments in the social sciences and philosophy of language supported this line of thinking. It was by now established in philosophy that a sentence possessed meaning and that the meaning expressed the intentions of the author(s). Even if this general attitude works when talking about the Bible, it fails miserably when applied to human products. This became painfully evident when people like Marx, Freud and others came along. Marx said that our intentions were defined by false consciousness, or by our unconscious class interests; Freud went further and saw our intentions guided by subconscious instincts.

What do such ideas do to texts and their meanings? They shape our attitude and mould the way we go about with texts and their meanings, of course. In what way? It has become common sense that people write texts to express their intentions, which are mostly '*impure or nefarious intentions*'. Unknown to us, our intentions are formed, shaped, and directed by class or caste interests. Our intentions merely aim to gratify our strivings for sex, money, power, or status. In India, it has become a huge industry to produce literature which says that a Brahminical 'conspiracy' underlies most of our cultural heritage and that the texts of the 'upper castes' merely express 'intentions' to dominate, oppress and cheat. Many Indologists have tried to 'show' that Vedic texts are 'clever, cunning and successful' strategies of Brahmins to oppress people. From here, it is but a truly short step to come up with the conclusion that every text is an interpretation, and that there are only interpretations, and no texts.

SAMPRADAYA, PARAMPARE AND TRADITIO

In Indian languages, we use *sampradaya and parampara* to indicate two phenomena distinct from each other, even though they are often used as synonyms. We can broadly characterize their difference in the following way: *sampradaya* mostly refers to the customs and practices of a social unit. This unit can be a group or a collective, big or small. Thus, we speak of the *sampradaya* of a family, or of the Vaishnava *Sampradaya*. *Parampara* localizes individual units by tracing lineages or relations. For instance, the *Guru-Shishya parampara* localizes a single individual and traces the relationship between a teacher and his pupils. This lineage can easily nestle within a *sampradaya*. An individual belonging to the Madhava or Vaishnava *Sampradaya* can claim an *acharya parampara* by tracing the routes to a teacher. Here, what is traced is a knowledge route: Guru is the teacher from whom the pupil has learnt. Even this rough explication is enough for us to go further: when multiple *sampradayas* and multiple *paramparas* coexist, generically one can speak of following the ways and means sanctioned by their *sampradaya* or *parampara*. Because both are assumed to conform to *shastras*, what is prescribed is *shastric*. The appellation applies to knowledge domains, including arts like music (for instance, Shastriya Sangeetha). Though more must be said about each of these, I will not go there for the time being. All we need to note is that in English we use 'tradition' to refer to both.

This English word comes from the Latin word '*traditio*', and as the Ancient Romans used it, referred to ancestral practices transmitted over generations to posterity. What one inherited from one's fathers and forefathers was *traditio* and to keep faith with the ancestors was to follow inherited practices. To the Romans, having a *traditio* meant having a *religio* (from which we get the English word 'religion'). As Christianity emerged in the milieu of Ancient Rome, its aggressive and combative stance towards Roman 'religions' also began to take shape. One of the criticisms that Ancient Roman thinkers had against Christianity was that, as a *new religion*, it was not a tradition (i.e., it was not an ancestral practice, as Romans understood *religio*). Christianity was neither faithful to Jewish practices nor was it the ancestral practice of any other peoples. Christianity's rejection of ancient practices made them *atheists* in the eyes of the Romans. In their fight against the Roman *religio*, the Christian response was to *reconfigure* what it meant to be a *'traditio'*. Instead of the ancestral practices of a people, *traditio* now signalled something entirely different (if the transformation from *traditio* to *religio* interests you, then read the second chapter of *'The Heathen in His Blindness...'*, 1994).

The contemporary English word 'tradition' has that core reference which Christianity supplied to *'traditio'* millennia ago. What is it? The Church said that it was safeguarding, nurturing, and transmitting *'the apostolic tradition'*. The pivot of this tradition and its centre of gravity is the *message of Christ*. The Apostles had heard Christ; they recorded his teachings. Peter, one of the Apostles, was 'the rock' on which the Church was founded. The message of Christ was entrusted to the Church. Thus, the apostolic tradition is about *interpreting* the Gospels. The Church alone can read, understand, and interpret the Bible because it has the authority of the tradition behind her. Not only the 'what' but also the 'how' of reading the Bible is true if and only if sanctioned by tradition. Otherwise, one would misunderstand the Bible or be guided into false readings by the Devil. Therefore, lay persons were not allowed to read the Bible; it existed only in Latin; only religious persons could comment on the Bible or write commentaries on the Church Fathers. In short, *tradition now refers to the permissible interpretations and meanings of a text.* This is how Christianity transfigured the Roman *traditio*, which originally referred to ancestral practices.

The Protestants in their turn, when challenging the Catholic Church, rejected many of its claims. By postulating an unmediated and direct relationship between God and the individual believer, people like Luther and Calvin cried out: *sola scriptura*! (Scripture alone!) According to them, to read, interpret or understand the Bible, no tradition is required; every believer could do so aided by the Almighty. Hence, they began to translate the Latin Bible into other languages (English, German, French, etc.). The Catholic Church did not take this lying down, of course. They challenged the Protestants: "If you read the Bible on your own outside the tradition, how do you know that you are not guided by the Devil? Is the influence you perceive that of God or of the Devil? What if you confuse God's truth with the Devil's lies?" These questions generated religious wars in Europe fuelled by militant debates about these issues. However, throughout its fight with the Catholic church, the Protestant Reformation did not shift the reference of the word 'tradition' – it *continued* to refer to the message (i.e., the meaning of texts), which required the apostolic tradition to decipher.

Soon, Biblical hermeneutics came into existence as a domain of learning. Lessons drawn from reading, understanding, and interpreting the Bible were transferred to other texts (after all, the Bible is also a text) and became 'textual hermeneutics'. This cluster of rules, assumptions and precepts, at times, is also called 'the hermeneutic tradition'. The British brought this approach to texts with them when they came to India. Thus, we speak of the 'Indian hermeneutic tradition', 'Indian textual traditions' etc. But when we do that, we also walk into a maze of new problems.

This happens when we *unreflectively* relate 'tradition' to our *sampradaya* and *parampara*. Even though we continue to differentiate the two, if our approach to Indian texts faithfully follows the Christian use, *even when ignorant of Christianity*, we will be trapped by the *logic(s) of language use*.

TEXTS AND HERESIES

Consider the fact that the Sanskrit language generated very systematic reflections on language and meaning much before such exercises occurred elsewhere in the world. Grammar was not only a particularly important subject – so was correct speaking, writing and style. Sanskrit is strict about the use of words and their meaning; it also developed construction rules for words and word-meanings instead of building dictionaries. That is, the speakers of this language formulated linguistic rules to understand meanings of words and sentences instead of seeking meaning primarily in authorial intentions or uses. Of course, people expressed their hopes, fears, and dreams – in other words, their intentions – through language and appropriate linguistic units. But when we answer the question, "what did the author intend?", we mostly speak about what the author is trying to say or do. However, 'intention' is not about the texts but rather about why the author writes what he does. When Indian culture claims that the Vedas are not authored by anyone, that makes it impossible to ask questions about authorial intentions. "Why were the Vedas enunciated?" is more difficult to answer than the question "why did God call Moses to Mount Sinai?", or "why did Jesus of Nazareth come to earth?", or "why is Christ necessary?", or "why did God reveal Himself in the Book?", and so on. God's word, the Bible, itself answers these questions. However, consider the following question: "Why do the Rig and the Sama Veda have so many identical passages?" Or "why was the Veda not written down, but did it remain oral even when script was discovered?" Where should we look for answers?

Our Vedic texts do not raise or answer such questions, though many Indologists do.

Furthermore, most of the texts in our culture have acquired authors only recently. Even where the author is named by the inherited tradition, it is very often unclear who that is: which Badarayana authored the Brahma Sutra, if indeed, one person authored it? Who is Gautama Akshapada, the author of Nyaya Sutra? Did Vyasa compose the entire Mahabharata or is what we have an accumulation over the centuries? Was there ever a Manu writing the Manava Dharmashastra or is it a compilation work undertaken by many people, or was it reconstructed by multiple redactors over many centuries? One of the facts that has had Western Indologists in a tizzy is precisely this question: who wrote it and why? If these issues were important to the Indian traditions, it is inexplicable why dating, authorship and, derivatively, intention are so *inconsequential.*

There is a second absence that is more significant. Despite the enormous emphasis on meaning in Sanskrit, despite the innumerable tendencies and traditions present in our culture, despite sharp disagreements and polemics between people, despite all these, our culture – and by extension Asian culture – does not know of heresies. Shankara and Madhva, to take just two Acharyas, differ from each other on most issues and are as opposed to each other's views as is possible. Yet, Madhva did not consider Shankara a heretic; none of the pupils and students of Shankara ever criticized Madhva for teaching heresies. People do not end up in hell because they follow these teachers. These two great minds 'interpreted' the same texts very differently and opposed each other's reading of the Upanishads, the Brahma Sutra and the Gita. And yet, no one calls the other a heretic or 'false'. Madhva thinks that Shankara is wrong. But he does not say that *Shankara propagates falsehood.* Heresy is about propagating falsehood as the truth. Indian culture does not know of heresy, while the Church, of course, considers itself to be the sole custodian of truth.

We must broaden this example. Throughout Asia, including India, people have interpreted Buddha's dialogues in astoundingly different ways. Yet even where each Buddhist tradition considers itself to be correct and all others wrong, there is no 'heresy' and no heretics. Each Buddhist follows the Buddha freely while knowing that others follow the Buddha in entirely different ways, including opposed ways. Yet, they do not become anxious; nor do they consider the others as the enemy. Even where they have sharp polemics with each other, there is no accusation of heresy.

This powerful negative evidence exhibits its true power when we contrast this with Christianity and Islam. In the Catholic interpretations of the Gospels, the Protestants only see the hand of the Devil; the Catholics considered Protestants as heretics; the Church has declared any number of interpretations as anathema. In this battle of interpretations, only one interpretation is and can be true; all others are wrong, misguided and false. This fight between truth and falsehood in certain matters is absent in India.

This does not mean that Indians believe in multiple truths. That is nonsense. Relativism with respect to truth, of course, can become a respectable option under certain conditions. However, the stance, 'to each his own truth' is a modern disease and is not to be found in the DNA of Indian culture. The notions of truth in India are as robustly absolutist as possible.

My suggestion is that the Indian ideas about meaning, understanding and language are different from what we take for granted today. Understanding the Upanishad or the Gita or the Buddha has little to do with an interpretation that allegedly gives us the true meaning of the teachings or the truth about the author's intentions.

TRUTH, KNOWLEDGE AND ADHIKARA

Today we witness a peculiar attitude among some people that involves a strange turn of phrase. Guided by a partially justified criticism of Indological scholarship, they argue that Indians have *adhikara* (authority) that Western intellectuals do not have. At times, the focus is on language, Sanskrit; at other times, it is about texts of Indian culture written in Sanskrit. This claim raises the following questions: on what exactly do Indians have *adhikara? What is the source of this adhikara?* (Or: from where does this *adhikara* come?)

Based on the short sketch in the previous pages, we can say that the authority of the Roman Catholic Church rests on what Jesus Christ as the only son of the Christian God said and did. How do we know what the Christ figure said or did? Well, we have the Apostles who witnessed, chronicled, and transmitted the acts of Christ. They were also commanded by Jesus to propagate the Good News. Thus, the Church has the authority on everyone who believes in the Bible and draws this authority from the Almighty Himself. It has the authority to guide the flock; it has the authority to deliver the message (because only those ordained by her can read the Bible) and its language (the Catholic Bible is preached in local languages by the priests but is not translated from Latin); and so on. In this message, God reveals Himself and *because He is the truth*, the message is true. The Church, as the bride of Christ, is the custodian and guardian of *this truth* on Earth, until the Christ's second coming. Because it has authority over truth on earth, the dogmas of the Church are the truth. Hence, when the Catholics say that tradition is required to find the truth, we can understand them, even if we disagree.

You must understand how deep and how far this authority reaches. Suppose we use the Aristotelean notion of truth ('to state the truth is to say what is the case') and hold it rigidly tied to sentences – meaning that truth is a linguistic property of sentences. Even then, the

Biblical interpretation, i.e., the meaning of Biblical words, phrases, and sentences falls under the authority of the Church. Of course, this is applicable only to a Catholic. No matter what you personally think the phrase from John's Gospel 'truth sets us free' means, if you are a Catholic, you must unconditionally accept what the Church says it means. The apostolic tradition gives this authority to the Church. Now, you must understand that this is what the word 'authority' means whether in English or in any other European language: *it is unconditional and brooks no disobedience in its domain.* This is also how the word 'authority' is used in Law, in the courts, in political science, in sociology, etc.

Now assume that I see the four Vedas as our 'holy books' or our 'scriptures'. Veda is also considered *apaurusheya*. Here, we will understand it to mean that it is not humanly authored. Does anyone have the 'scriptural authority' to claim what the words, phrases, and sentences of Vedic texts can or cannot mean? The Vedic texts do not delegate authority to any person or organization, the way the Gospels do. The Christian Gospels are not silent on this important issue of authority. If this *adhikara* is important, why are the Vedas silent about it? One possible answer is that this idea is not native to our culture. It is borrowed.

Some people claim that the Veda was denied to the Shudras and other 'oppressed' people by the 'cunning and conspiratorial' Brahmins. Let us look at this scandal too, which is not only alleged to be a blot on our culture but is apparently also deeply rooted in 'Hinduism', the so-called majority religion of India.

What exactly is the nature of this Veda that was allegedly denied to some? The consensus among the recent 'authoritative' translators of the Rig Veda is that it is the *first religious praise poetry of mankind.* 'Religious' because it is about all kinds of *Devatas*; 'poetry' because its verses follow specific meters; 'praise poetry' because its content is full of praises of the *devatas* (how glorious they are; how heroic they are…) and of 'tribal chiefs' from whom the composers of the Veda expected gifts if their praise met with the satisfaction of the tribal chieftain. The Rig Veda consists of hardly much else besides this. In that case, who fusses about teaching it? Besides, why bother learning it? According to the Western Indologists, all one *can* 'learn' is to recite praises of some unknown tribal chiefs in the hope of receiving some *bakshish*. So, what exactly has been denied to the oppressed classes by the nefarious and cunning Brahmins? Are the 'revolutionaries' up in arms because Shudras were not taught to recite *praise poetry*?

There is a reason to formulate the question this way. Consider the fact that Vedic Sanskrit had many terms, including words for poetry. *Stotra*, *stuti* (praise), *kavya*, were genres known and in use during that period. This being the case, why did the Ancients use '*Veda*' (meaning 'knowledge') to refer to these collections of verses? Why did they not call it *Kavya* or *Stuti* or whatever else? Whatever their reason, they thought that this collection of verses had to do with knowledge and helped in the emergence of knowledge. This item, 'knowledge', was particularly important to our culture and it continues to be. It is valued more highly than truth. Truth, in our culture, is subordinated to knowledge. In one sense, what could make the Vedas 'holy' is their assumed connection to knowledge. Saraswathi embodies knowledge which is why she is 'sacred' or 'holy'.

The above considerations lead in the following direction. Indian culture does not and cannot countenance anybody having authority over Saraswathi. Neither a mortal nor any divinity has any *adhikara* over Saraswathi. Therefore, Indian culture could never entertain the idea of *adhikara over knowledge*. An agent has *adhikara* over his actions (karma); in a narrow sense of dharma, we can speak of a *dharmadhikari*; when it is seen as law, we can speak of a *Nyayadhipathi* or of a *Nyayadhisha*. But we cannot and do not allow *adhikara* over *gyaana* to anyone. A *gyaanadhipathi* has no authority over *gyaana* but only over its transmission to the deserving.

Now, we can couple the two issues together. If none has authority over knowledge, Indians have no special adhikara, when compared to their Western counterparts. By the same token, none had or has the authority to deny knowledge to the 'oppressed'.

CHAPTER 19

TRANSLATING WORDS

Many express concern that the English translations of some words from Indian languages distort the meanings of these words. If we restrict ourselves to terms like *deva, dharma* and the like, the worry is not just that their translations distort their meanings but also that something different or alien by way of reference and meaning emerges that does not exist in the source language.

With respect to some of these words, we can build a reasonable case in defence of the above stance. That is because there is at least some theory about religion that we accept (however provisional such an acceptance might be) using which we can show that '*deva*' or '*devata*' cannot be translated as 'God'. So far so good.

Could we generalize this point to say that this is a special issue about Sanskrit and, by corollary, our culture? Such an attempt faces two kinds of problems: (a) Are all translations from one language into another folly? Saying 'yes' to this question is so absurdly parochial that no one would take us seriously. The very idea that contributions from a language or a culture are contributions to humanity would be undercut. So, we must allow that some transformation of the meanings of words in the process of translation is inevitable. (b) We need to put restrictions on translations regarding only some words from the source language and, in each case, we must give a reasoned defence of our stance. How are we going to defend these restrictions in a reasonable way?

The first way of doing so is to appeal to a theory that some of us accept and build arguments on that basis. Note, however, that the acceptance of a theory is itself subject to certain cognitive constraints; not every set of sentences can be called a 'theory we accept'. Today, we know something about human knowledge and the status of scientific theories. Such theories do not exist for most words we use in Sanskrit or our other native languages. For instance, such is the case for the word 'dharma'. We know of no theory of dharma that meets the cognitive criteria that we expect a scientific theory to meet.

Where we do not have an explicit theory to help us, there we can appeal to something like an 'intuitive theory' that cultures transmit to their members. Has the Indian culture of today transmitted an ability that allows us to make intuitive sense of some of these words? Here is where, I am afraid, the shoe is going to pinch. I think that *it has not*. In one area at least, we are as clueless as any Westerner!

Consider the following words we effortlessly use, while talking about human beings: *'ahamkara', 'chitta', 'manas', 'bhavana', 'raaga-dvesha'* and their kin. Bracket away for the time being what you have learnt about these words from texts authored by people like Patanjali or Abhinavagupta or Shankarachaarya because millions upon millions of people use these words without having read such texts. Having done that, ask yourself the following questions: What is *manas*? What does it refer to in the human psychology that you intuitively know? What is *chitta*? What is the difference between *buddhi, manas* and *chitta*? Is there a difference between *manobhaavana* and *manovikaara*? Is *chittashuddhi* required when we have *manovikaara*? If yes, *chitta* and *manas* refer to the same entity; if no, what is the difference? Was Duryodhana an *ahamkari* or a *durahamkari*? What is the difference between the two? How do you identify these two states as being different?

It is my claim that we are as clueless here as any Westerner. What a Westerner learns from studying a Patanjali or an Abhinavagupta is also what you can learn from them, taking individual cognitive differences into account, of course. The cards are stacked in favour of the Westerner because his understanding of his native language (say, English) is deeper than your knowledge of English. He at least possesses an intuitive psychology that tells him that these concepts are 'different from and alien to' those he is familiar with. His 'intuitive' psychology has absorbed ideas from many domains of social science – from psychology through law to philosophy. We lack the intuitive access he has. In our case, we are also deceived: because we use these words *unreflectively* (in this sense, proficiently) we are deceived into believing that we know what these words mean and what they refer to. *We do not.*

If this is true, it reveals another layer of colonial consciousness. We have taken to English the way ducks take to water because we do not intuitively know what words from our own languages mean! This is why the earlier generations of Indians did not object to the translations of the British: we knew neither what 'dharma' meant, nor do we know what 'normative ethics' means. Our understanding of *Ishwara* or *Brahma* (be it 'nirguna' or 'saguna') is as shallow as our understanding of God.

There are many, many, implications to what I am saying. One is relevant for our purposes: *discussions about how and whether we should translate Sanskrit words into English do not arise from an understanding of our culture and traditions but from ignorance.* Unlike 'atom', 'genes' or 'quark', the words I am talking about refer to our conception of human beings. Do we not need such conceptions to think meaningfully about ourselves and talk meaningfully about others?

Consider the possibility that these terms are entirely technical, i.e., they are specific terms in a developed theory. In that case, in the absence of knowledge of these theories, there is no way to make sense of these words. Let us assume that we have access to some or another intuitive (not explicit) model or theory of human beings using which we make sense of ourselves and others. Even in that case, the words we use in our daily lives remain technical terms in Indian texts. We do not use other notions from our intuitive theories and models about human beings, assuming the presence of such words. Then, our intuitive theories might as well be non-existent. We use (technical) words we do not understand; we do not use words (that might be present in the intuitive models), which we might understand.

The second possibility is that we do not possess 'silent' theories about ourselves and the world. Then, the consequences are still the same: we use words we do not understand to make sense of ourselves and other human beings. If I am not a physicist, translating 'atom' as the smallest particle of matter will not disorient me. However, whatever my profession, I cannot go about in the world without concepts to think about myself, my wife and kids, and other human beings. If I use words that I do not understand for this purpose, I end up not understanding myself, my wife and children, and my surroundings.

Given the fundamental importance of words like *buddhi, manas, ahamkara* and so on to our daily lives, it is not sufficient that there exists a community of specialists somewhere, who can only explain what an Abhinavagupta or a Shankara said. Even if they tell me what *manas* means in Sanskrit, how do I identify that entity in myself? Is my desire for a masala dosa expressed by my *manas* or *buddhi* or is it a *vikaara* of one or both these entities? When I feel like punching someone, what prevents me: *buddhi, chitta, manas, dharma,* or, as Gandhi puts it, our 'conscience'? What do I need to change in me or train in me if I need to improve and learn to become a better human being? How do I identify those entities? How do I know what trains them? Your experts will have to appeal to words I already know to explain what *buddhi* or *manas* is to me. But then, what are some of those words I should already know to understand these experts? Besides, I need to apply them. In my everyday living, I need to identify whether *manas* and *buddhi* are different or whether they are the same, whether I have *ahamkara* or not and so on.

I am not comparing the alleged scientific temperament in the West to our lack of knowledge. I say that your average Joe knows what he approximately means by ego, concentration, attention, determination, etc., when he uses these words in his daily intercourse with people. I am saying that *we* cannot do this: all the words we use and the only ones we know are the so-called 'technical terms'. Their meanings are known to specialists in Sanskrit reading technical treatises.

Think of words like 'culture', 'religion', 'race', 'will', etc. They are called 'essentially contested concepts' in the literature indicating that people have many disputes about the meaning of these concepts and that there is no consensus about the definition of these words. By virtue of the absence of such a consensus, their usage in daily language is fluid. A word like *manas* also shares these properties. But there is something more in our case than these 'essentially contested concepts'.

Even if one does not know what 'will' means, what 'God' means, what mind or its relation to the brain is, there are institutions and practices that lend meaning to these words in the West. There is the apparatus of the judiciary that lends meaning to 'will'; there is the church and religious institutions; there is the talk and structure of human rights; there are any number of ongoing reflections about the nature of mind and brain and the nature of personal identity. In sum, there are a whole host of practices current in Western culture that give technical meanings to these words which then percolate downwards in society through several institutions like the media, schools, universities and so on. This is absent in India.

This is not all. We use words from Western common sense without sharing or having that common sense to translate and understand Indian words! "*Manas* is mind", we say, knowing neither what mind is nor what *manas* is; "He has a strong personality", we say, knowing neither what a 'person' is, nor what the strength of personality means and not at all knowing what a *vyakti* is and whether this word can be used to translate 'person' or not. We coin words in Hindi and other languages to translate technical terms from Western theories: liberalism, secularism, social justice, democracy, stereotypes, and so on, when we neither understand the Indian language terms nor the theories about these concepts written in European languages.

Take, 'freedom' as an example. Without blushing, we translate Rousseau's statement "Man is born free" into Indian languages without even understanding that this sentence does not make any sense in Indian culture or in any of its languages. We think 'freedom' means *svatantra*: you would not make such a silly claim, if only you knew what 'freedom' or *svatantra* mean. We translate 'democracy' as *praja parbhutva* with the understanding that 'citizens' means *praja* when we neither know nor care whether *prabhu* is different from *vibhu* and what either of the two terms means.

The issue of 'freedom' is central in philosophy, in moral theories, in political theories about State and society, in legal theories, and psychological theories, etc. If you were to blandly state what the issue is in a single sentence it would be: it is a good thing for people to be free and everyone 'ought' to be free. In ethical theories, for instance, a moral action is an action of choice, made freely without coercion. In fact, in the absence of freedom, morality is not possible. Let me draw a contrast between this way of thinking, which only appears to be true based on universal consent, and our ideas about 'karma' and 'rebirth'. You need not assume the truth of *punarjanma* in order to follow my point. If the fruits of one's action do not track (very strictly) the agent across several lives, the idea of both karma and rebirth become senseless. Somehow, these notions are a part of our Indian understanding of morality. That means to say, if there was no binding and strict determinism, ethics is impossible. *Here is, then, the contrast: according to Western culture, moral action is impossible if it is not free; according to us, without strict determinism, moral action is impossible.* Yet, how many of us do not act as though freedom is a self-explanatory concept? Do you know where the origins of this problem lie? God created Man and gave him the freedom to choose between God and the Devil. In secularized terms, between good and evil. The possibility of salvation, that is, of being saved from the clutches of the Devil, depend on this free 'choice'. Therefore, theological issues arose: What does human freedom mean? Why did God give us freedom? Are we condemned to be free? Our *svatantra* does not mean freedom as its contrast term *paratantra* indicates. Our gods are *sarva tantra svatantra*, i.e., beings for whom all tantras are their own (*sva*). What exactly are we doing then, when we have discussions about a 'free society', 'freedom of individuals', etc.?

I trust I have been able to show that we neither understand the technical or theoretical terms we use in our daily intercourse nor the English words we translate into our native languages. However, we are convinced that we know both India and the West!

CHAPTER 20

OUR TASK IN THE 21ST CENTURY

If you have been with me so far, you will have realized that one of the most intriguing aspects of Indian culture is the knowledge it produces: knowledge which emerges through systematic reflection on human experience. Our experiences are many: no one set, no one kind of experience exhausts what we go through. We have purely personal experiences of the world such as our ambitions, hopes, dreams, and frustrations, and entirely social ones relating to the sorrow and injustice that other beings in the world experience. So, knowledge that reflects on and systematizes such experiences presupposes multiple learning sites, many diverse perspectives, and varied kinds of intellectual skills.

You have now had a glimpse of the filters and difficulties facing us. We need to plot the rich and varied contours of these filters and the processes which create and sustain them. When we do so, we will have initiated a revolution in human thinking: at last, one will be able to begin to speak in terms of the *sciences* of the social. Until such stage, all we have are bad Christian theologies *masquerading* as 'social sciences'.

If Indian culture encouraged the production of such knowledge, it also gave birth to people capable of teaching these skills (call them skills for the sake of convenience) to others to help them knowledgeably go about in the world. Anyone and everyone who was willing to learn this was taught; everyone capable of learning produced such knowledge. What exactly was taught when people were taught to think about their experiences? How were these abilities taught and retaught over generations, across the whole of India? These are the important but ill-understood questions of today.

Two factors are of importance here, for now. One: reflection on experience was itself taught experientially (a better word would be 'practically') because the results of such reflection which transform experience can only be experiential. Our traditions did not write 'how to' manuals even though most of what they wrote are practical manuals. Two: we cannot understand them properly today because of more than one thousand years of colonial consciousness. The contribution of colonialism was to provide us with a pair of spectacles with which we are born: all these manuals from our ancestors appear to us as vague 'philosophies', esoteric 'spirituality', or mystical 'advices'. We cannot even imagine that a Shankara or a Buddha did not write tracts in philosophy or metaphysics but that they may have belonged to some other domain of knowledge; we do not see how a Brahmasutra or a Bhagavadgita or a Yogasutra could be considered a 'theory' about the world.

At the same time, we also inherit the modern-day world. We are students of scientific theories and technological achievements. In whatever form or fashion we do, we are learning to do scientific research and to build theories. We are also learning the need to distinguish between scientific theories and non-scientific ones, and we also know that the sciences are one of the best examples of human knowledge.

In a way, this situation sets up both the context and the task for the intellectuals of India. Resuscitating Sanskrit words (the 'Indic categories') by digging into this or that tract or treatise will not even begin to address the problems we confront. In some senses, these so-called Indic categories are rapidly losing their semantic content to us, whether people from my generation or those from the younger generation. Writing tracts on 'Indian psychology' by culling the meaning of words from Sanskrit texts or by having various scholars summarize theories of Indian psychology as the Gita formulates it, or from Patanjali's Yoga Sutra, according to Advaita, and so on are curiosa that can only satisfy the ego of the writer or the publisher. What we need to do is to begin the process of reflecting on the Indian cultural experience, fashioning terms as we need them and reaching out to the past only so that we can identify whether their problems were like ours, and whether they formulated answers that would make sense to us in the twenty-first century. *Our task is to take up anew the challenge our culture posed and answered so successfully in the past: reflect on human experience and relate these reflections to experience so that the latter can be moulded, changed, formed, and transformed.*

To do so we must *re-establish our connection to Indian tradition and its way of teaching to reflect on human experience.* However, there is no direct way to do so. Out of sheer necessity, we must go through the prism of scientific theorizing. This is not only necessary but also desirable: we now need to develop ways of thinking about experience in a systematic fashion, and science, in the first place, is systematic thinking. Therefore, the social sciences can only be systematic reflections on human experiences. This means, in one and the same movement, we must bring together two threads which have developed independently: the practical way of teaching and thinking about human experience and a theoretical way of reflecting about Nature. Our road to the former is through the latter.

When we succeed, we will have brought two things together: to think practically about human experience by building theories about human experience. There is only one way to *transform life into a site of learning* and that is by pursuing a practical, scientific way. We must solve practically what has been a theoretical question in philosophy: the relation between theory and practice. In the process of making our past and its accumulated knowledge relevant for our present, in the process of answering the question what it means to be Indian, we will have given the world its first systematic sciences of the social.

CONCLUSION

One of the questions which has remained constant in the West is the following: 'What does it mean to be Christian?'; in Latin, *Quid sit Christianum esse?*

Someone, anyone, is a Christian if and only if he has the properties X, Y, Z. Such a discussion has been conducted during the two millennia that Christianity has been in existence by the different Christian sects. Each has called itself the 'true' Christianity and stipulated some conditions for being a "true Christian." This discussion is an internal problem within Christianity and their answers do not interest me, except in one way.

What I need to understand is why each sect within Christianity (from the Catholics through the Orthodox to the Protestants) finds it an important problem. That is, these facts constitute the problem-situation, assuming I want to produce knowledge about the phenomenon that Christianity is.

Even here, we know that Christianity is simultaneously several things: it is a movement of people, it is a landlord and shareholder, it is a marketing bureau and a political force... and it is also what it is to its believers, namely, the revelation of the Biblical God in Jesus of Nazareth. I am primarily interested in understanding Christianity in its last aspect, namely, as a specific religion. I do not want to claim that their beliefs are either illusions or true: my facts are their self-descriptions, which not only change from one sect to another but also over time.

Consequently, I set up a hypothesis about what religion is and how Christianity is also a religion. Using this hypothesis, I explain certain other features that are empirically observable in history.

If one must criticize me, one must follow the rules of the scientific game: to come up with an alternative hypothesis that not only explains everything I explain, but also more. In all honesty, I have yet to come across such a hypothesis. But I do fervently hope that such an explanation emerges in the future. (Those interested in the theory of religion question, read '*The Heathen in His Blindness...*', 1994).

Questions like 'what does it mean to be a Hindu?' or 'Why I am/am not a Hindu?' are pseudo variations of this question. This route is a dead end, and it provides non-answers. Although we may use the word 'Hindu' for the sake of convenience, one cannot perform the same operation on that word like one can with words like 'Christian' or 'Muslim' (evidenced by countless Indologist attempts to define 'Hinduism'). That is because we do not have a native religion in India. The only level at which we can understand that which exists in India is at the level of culture. *Indian culture.* Hence the question, what does it mean to be 'Indian'?

What does the question mean at the end of this journey of ours? It means that we must seek answers to this question in our experiences and in the transmitted ways of reflecting about them. Language, religion, region do not make us into 'Indians'. Our passports and ID cards do not make us into non-Indians: our Kerala Jews living as Israeli citizens today and the American doctors of Indian origin are as much Indians as they were when they lived in our cities and villages. What makes all of us into Indians is our culture. As I said earlier, culture is a configuration of learning and the differences between cultures must be tracked accordingly as how resources of socialization are used. In

India, it means talking about how Indians utilize these resources to form, modify, and direct the structuring of what they undergo. Thus, to be Indian today (and yesterday) involves this endless process of dealing thoughtfully with experience. In this process, one can speak only of degrees of proficiency: there is no perfect Indian. By the same token, there is no imperfect Indian either. In one sense, either you are an Indian or you are not. In another sense, the differences among Indians form a continuum of proficiency. It is because of this that we can *thinkingly* raise the question what it is to be Indian, without scare quoting the word 'Indian'.

In this book, I have simply shown why the question is meaningful and why it is not the same kind of question that 'identity' theorists from Calcutta to California raise. I am far from answering the question at this point in our journey. A day will come, I am sure, when the question gets answered satisfactorily. But that day is not yet there. Currently, it is in the future, waiting for those capable of doing justice to its depth. I will not be around to applaud the accomplishment, but I can relinquish the platform with at least some sense of hope today. More, I do not need for now.

SALUTATIO

Now, a word or two about dedicating this book to Quintus Aurelius Symmachus, who was the last non-Christian Prefect of Rome around the end of the fourth century. His experiences and the way he thought about them *aptly* track our past and our present nearly two thousand years later. In a letter to Emperor Valentinian the Second, Symmachus requests a space for the Romans to practice their own *traditions* without being persecuted by the aggressive religion that Christianity was. His plea was not granted, and his people have disappeared. His gods too are long forgotten. But his thoughts, from the other side of the globe, still ring true.

> *Grant, I beg you, that what in our youth we took over from our fathers, we may in our old age hand on to posterity. The love of established practice is a powerful sentiment...*

> *Everyone has his own customs, his own religious practices...If long passage of time lends validity to religious observances, we ought to keep faith with so many centuries, we ought to follow our forefathers who followed their forefathers and were blessed in so doing...And so we ask for peace for the gods of our fathers, for the gods of our native land. It is reasonable that whatever each of us worships is really to be considered one and the same.*

> *We gaze up at the same stars, the sky covers us all, the same universe compasses us. What does it matter what practical*

system we adopt in our search for truth? Not by one avenue only can we arrive at so tremendous a secret.

(Barrow, R. H., Trans., 1973, *Prefect and Emperor: The Relationes of Symmachus. A.D. 384.* Oxford: The Clarendon Press, Pp. 37-41; my italics.)

SELECTED READINGS

BOOKS:

- *"The Heathen in His Blindness…": Asia, the West and the Dynamic of Religion.* Leiden and New York: E.J. Brill (1994). Second and revised edition by Manohar, New Delhi, 2005.

- *Reconceptualizing India Studies.* New Delhi: Oxford University Press. 2012

- *Cultures Differ Differently.* New Delhi: Routledge. (Forthcoming, 2021).

ARTICLES/BOOK CHAPTERS:

- "Caste-based Reservation and Social Justice in India." In Martin Fárek et al. (Eds), *Western Foundations of the Caste System.* Basingstoke: Palgrave Macmillan, pp. 31-55. 2017.

- "Indian Culture and its Social Security System." *Journal of Contemporary Thought,* Special Number on Critical Humanities, 41 (2), Summer Issue, pp. 241-266. 2015.

- "Translation, Interpretation and Culture: On the Disingenuity of a Comparative Theology." *Canadian Social Science,* 10 (5), pp. 39-47. 2014.

- "On the Dark Side of the 'Secular': Is the Religious-secular Distinction a Binary?" *Numen – International Review for the History of Religions*, 61 (1), pp. 33-52. 2014.

- "Orientalism, Postcolonialism and the 'Construction' of Religion." In Esther Bloch, Marianne Keppens and Rajaram Hegde (Eds), *Rethinking Religion in India. The Colonial Construction of Hinduism*. London: Routledge, pp. 135-163. 2010.

- "What do Indians Need: A History or the Past?" *Dialogue*, 12 (1). 2010.

- "Spirituality in Management Theories: A Perspective from India." In Sharda Shirley Nandram, Margot Esther Borden (Eds.), *Spirituality and Business: Exploring Possibilities for a New Management Paradigm*. Heidelberg: Springer, pp. 45-59. 2009.

- "Why Understand the Western Culture?" In Nirmala Rao Khadpekar (Ed.), *Understanding Multiculturalism*. Hyderabad: The ICFAI University Press, pp. 184-195. 2008.

- With Esther Bloch and Jakob De Roover, "Rethinking Colonialism and Colonial Consciousness: The Case of Modern India." In S. Raval (Ed.), *Rethinking Forms of Knowledge in India: Critical Revaluations*. Delhi: Pencraft International, pp. 179-212. 2008.

- With Sarah Claerhout, "Are Dialogues Antidotes to Violence? Two Recent Examples from Hinduism Studies." *Journal for the Study of Religions and Ideologies*, 7 (19), pp. 118-143. 2008.

- "How to Speak for the Indian Traditions: An Agenda for the Future." *Journal of the American Academy of Religion*, 73 (4), pp. 987-1013. 2005.

- "We Shall Not Cease from Exploration": An invitation disguised as a position paper composed at the behest of Arena for the theme "Decolonizing Social Sciences". 1985.

WEBSITES:

- See S.N. Balagangadhara's academia.edu page for more writings (https://ugent.academia.edu/SNBalagangadhara)

- www.hipkapi.com Here, short writings of S.N. Balagangadhara and his students are collected and made accessible.

www.ingramcontent.com/pod-product-compliance
Lightning Source LLC
Chambersburg PA
CBHW031103250726
48655CB00004B/1568